Part 1

THE CHASE

Of Pursuit and Romance

The high school dream girl that got away,
Betty Conklin.

The one he loved first did not love him back.

They jitterbugged together and laughed together, and his heart leapt whenever he saw her, whenever he thought of her. But she did not love him back. This was the summer before his senior year of high school, and she had asked another boy on a hayride, and he would never be the same because of it. "I turned myself into a different guy," he would recall. This different guy was self-assured, a dapper fellow whose new wardrobe bespoke his reinvention—the jaunty flannel shirts, the yellow cords, the saddle shoes. He now wrote for the school paper under the byline Hep Hef. He also wrote songs and drew cartoon strips that chronicled the arc of his young life and his young loves. He learned then that he lived largely to be in love, to pine, or to yearn. He learned that his heart felt best when aflutter. Of this time, a classmate buddy of his later remembered: "His interest in girls was intense. Hef was constantly falling in love, one girl at a time, and would be smitten for maybe a month or so. If he wasn't in love, he felt incomplete and unhappy."

This would never change. The boy was father to the man he would become. And the man he would become loved women, one after another ad infinitum, with the wide-eyed

"WHEN AM I GONNA KISS YOU GOOD MORNING."

"HEARTACHES"

"THAT'S HOW MUCH I LOVE YOU, BABY."

"GUILTY"

"I GOT A GAL I LOVE."

"SEPTEMBER SONG."

"SENTIMENTAL REASONS"

"SOONER OR LATER"

"LINDA"

"ANNIVERSARY SONG"

"IT'S A GOOD DAY"

"THIS TIME"

"HOODLE ADDLE"

"HOW ARE THINGS IN GLOCCA MORA?"

"SEPTEMBER SONG."

"GUILTY"

MILLIE AND HEF AT COLONIAL MANOR'S FORMAL. THIS SNAP HAS BEEN TITLED "BEAUTY AND THE BEAST." MILLIE IS WEARING (FOR THE FIRST TIME) THE FORMAL HEF GAVE HER FOR HER 21ST BIRTHDAY.

exuberance of the boy in saddle shoes. As a man, he would be almost naive in love, giddy and intense—one friend aptly nicknamed him High School Harry, this in his fifth decade—and yet the ad infinitum would also make him aware in love. He would repeatedly declare: "My life has been a quest for a world where the words to the songs are true." He meant the love songs of yore, the dreamy ones, the ones Sinatra and Billie Holiday sang while caressing the microphone and suggesting bittersweet romance. Such romance had already been the foundation of his empire. Also, he would say, "For me, being in love is the very essence of being alive." And "I think life is deadly dull when a relationship becomes routine and boring." And "I admit that I'm still the same romantic pushover I was when I was young."

While there would be sexual adventures beyond reckoning and well-nigh-innumerable bedmates, he always pursued primary relationships that filled him with fierce longing (even while openly straying therein; he did, after all, have a reputation of epic proportions to uphold). He had romanticized his first marriage to high school sweetheart Mildred Williams until he realized that the romance had faded, that he was not built for marriage after all: "It was a period of dreams lost, dreams set aside—trying to follow a different road, a road not charted in my own terms." He created *Playboy* so as to re-create himself, just as he had done at Steinmetz High School in Chicago. His magazine gave him license to play again, and his long-term playmates in the decades that followed—his Special Ladies, as he would call them—gave him reason to swoon head over slippers. He said in the autumn of 1968, at age forty-two, "I'd rather meet a girl and fall in love, and have her fall in love with me, than earn another hundred million."

In fact he had met that girl months earlier on the set of his syndicated television show *Playboy After Dark.* She was a petite eighteen-year-old coed who resembled the one he had loved first, the one who did not love him back. This girl, however, *would* love him back, famously so. Her name was Barbara Klein, whom he would rename Barbi Benton in the pages of *Playboy.* Over the next eight years she would become the extra-special lady that people thought of most whenever they thought of Hef in love. "Barbi became a kind of Hollywood version of the teenage romance I never really had when I was in high school," he said later. "I was crazy about her." On the night that they met, he danced with her to the song "This Guy's in Love with You." He softly sang the lyrics into her ear and, as ever, believed those lyrics were true.

*W*hen You Know for Sure, You Know for Sure

I asked Barbi out the first night we met. "But I've never been out with anyone over twenty-four," she said. "That's okay," I replied. "Neither have I."

———————

*B*eing in Love Feels Far Better
Than Not Being in Love

Everything changes when you're in love. The food tastes better. The music is sweeter. Everything is a little more delicious because you're sharing it with somebody you care about.

If you are a romantic, I think it's possible to fall in love with somebody across a crowded room. Essentially, love is an illusion. It's something you project. And it has a great deal to do with what love, or youthful fantasies of love, came before. We tend to repeat ourselves and fall in love with variations on the same person over and over again. If you think about it, you'll know what I mean.

"A romantic relationship for me is an escape from the challenges and problems I face in my work," he once said. "It's a psychological and emotional island I slip away to." Rarely has he been cast adrift from any such island for very long, as he indicated in a memo to his attorney in early 1988: "Throughout the 1960s, 1970s and 1980s I have had a series of serious romantic, live-in relationships that included Cynthia Maddox, 1961–1963; Mary Warren, 1963–1967; Barbi Benton, 1969–1976; Sondra Theodore, 1976–1981; Shannon Tweed, 1981–1983; and Carrie

7

Leigh, 1983–January 1988." The reason for the memo, incidentally, was in response to a misbegotten and quickly dropped $35 million palimony suit filed by Carrie Leigh, the most tempestuous and sexually omnivorous of all the Special Ladies who had inhabited a Playboy Mansion with him. (To wit: "All of these women knew full well that there was little or no possibility that I would ever consider marrying again," he had added.) The point being, he is lousy at alone and worse than ever when not in love.

Thus it was in January 1988, two weeks after Miss Leigh had left him under a thundercloud of false accusations (no matter that she had for years been taking other lovers in wide variety), that Cupid drew bow upon him once more. The Playmate of that Very Month of that Very Year happened to be boarding at the Mansion Guest House while working on a pictorial with photographer Helmut Newton. Her name was Kimberley Conrad—a blonde, twenty-four-year-old no-nonsense "Alabama-born, Vancouver-bred angel" (per Hef)—upon whom he had cast his wide High School Harry eyes and all of a sudden sensed renewal attendant. She rebuffed his invitations to a pair of Mansion Movie Nights—French art films, no less—until he approached her once again after the second movie ended, as she lounged on his lavish premises. "I told her that I was really interested in her and would like to spend some time with her," he would recall. "And she said, 'Well, I don't really know you.' And I said, 'How are

Mr. Playboy attempts the Improbable: taking Kimberley Conrad to be his "Playmate for a Lifetime."

you going to get to know me if we don't spend some time together?'" (Hef's line!) "And that line, the simple logic of it—from that moment on, everything changed! We spent that evening together. If this had been a movie, that night there would have been strings and perhaps a little Bobby Hackett horn."

On July 1 of the following year, she became the second Mrs. Hugh Marston Hefner. Certain lines apparently work better than others.

It's Not What You Say in a Pickup Line but What You Don't Say

The best line is really not a line. The best line is listening. That is to say: The best way of getting a woman interested in you is to be interested in her. Look for some kind of common connection.

On the other hand, however, I've also had a lot of luck by simply saying "My name is Hugh Hefner," but that may not work for everyone.

Try Not to Try Too Hard

You are never at your best when it really matters, because you are too cautious. Ironically, I think you're at your best in the beginning of the relationships that don't matter as much to you, when there isn't too much at stake. You are at your worst when it really counts.

Just try to relax and take it one step at a time.

Say It When You Know It— As Long As You Truly Believe It

Tell her that you love her as soon as you think it's true. There's nothing wrong with wearing your heart on your sleeve.

The best thing that you can bring to a relationship is what you're really thinking and feeling. The worst thing in a relationship is deception and game-playing.

Eagerness in love would always be both his blessing and curse. It had failed him with his fateful high school crush —her name, by the way, was Betty Conklin—although he harbored vestiges of that crush for years to come. (Poetically, five decades after high school, as his marriage to Kimberley Conrad unraveled, it was Betty Conklin that he kissed—platonically, of course—at the stroke of midnight to welcome in January 1, 1998, when she came to his annual Mansion New Year's Eve bacchanal.) "Betty represented to me the fulfillment of all my boyhood dreams," he would note. "I projected everything that I was interested in, everything I had observed in my life, all the dreams that I had extracted from movies, all of this onto her. She couldn't possibly have lived up to that. It was an illusion."

The dreams he projected onto Barbi Benton, however, would stick better, if only because he became wise enough to learn some patience. While there was a twenty-four-year age difference stacked against them, patience and a knack for playing games of the heart only emboldened his resolve to capture hers. For instance, she wouldn't allow him to bring her back to his Sunset Boulevard penthouse alone: "That would've been a mistake! I had high morals and didn't want to be taken advantage of, so I thought that the best way to avoid that was to go out and be among people with him." He played along, didn't push too hard, even acceded to her unwillingness to let him pick her up at her UCLA dormitory (in his limousine, natch) for their dates. "I always drove my own car to meet him at restaurants or clubs," she would say. "But whatever he was doing, he was charming me. He had much more charm than the boys I saw in college. He was wonderful and cute, even though I thought he was too old."

This Guy's in Love with Barbi Benton.

Then, too, there was the matter of her virginity, which she had no intention of relinquishing any time soon. Two of his earlier major loves, Cynthia Maddox and Mary Warren, along with scores of other young women, had also presented him with the same challenge, which usually culminated in the same result. Feelings intensified, as they are wont to, and walls changed to portals, as his gentleness would impress each woman he ever knew. Of Barbi, he said, "So I waited months. I didn't want to scare her away." She came to Chicago in February 1969 for what would be their first Valentine's Day together. His secretary had shown him his horoscope for that day; "it said something encouraging about consummating an affair," he recalled. That night they spun on his Round Rotating Bed in his Master's Quarters and made love for the first time, as only a romantic would have it. Said Barbi: "It was too late to turn back. It was like, Now is the night."

Hefner Versus Freud:
It's Not About a Cigar, Really

Women want the same things men want. They want to be loved and taken care of—emotionally and in other ways. They want a relationship that permits them to grow.

———————

*H*ere Is Why You Want Her

What makes women sexy is partly physical image and partly what they're thinking—how they manage to express it in both appearance and what they say. A woman who thinks sexy is likely to appear sexy. It has a lot to do with spirit and attitude. That, combined with vulnerability, can be tremendously appealing. A woman you want to both protect and possess is perhaps the sexiest woman of all.

There Are Rules to the Game, Most Unfortunately

There's a danger in the early part of a relationship: If you appear to care too much, sometimes a girl may back away. She may often be more attracted to somebody who she thinks is hard to get—just as a guy often is. Of course there's nothing rational about that. As a matter of fact, it's counterproductive. But it's a reality. Unfortunately, it then becomes a game, which means you have to sometimes hold back true feelings to keep her from running away.

Too many guys pay too much attention to what they have on their own minds and miss the cues and clues that may establish a common connection. Don't just think about what you're feeling; think about what responses you're getting and are likely to elicit from what you say and do. The key to it all is not simply following your heart, but paying attention and listening.

Blondes are his weakness: There would, of course, be a blonde preponderance throughout his life—every hue of gold and yellow and flax, from platinum to strawberry to dusky to dirty and all shades in between. In particular, after his separation from the blonde Kimberley Conrad Hefner, he seemed to specialize exclusively in the tint. Blonde posses of three or six or eight would flank him in public and share his vast bed in private. His fascination with blondness—the shimmer and spice and allure of it—began as most of his yearnings had: at the movies, at the Mont-clare Theater on the West Side of Chicago, where a young and impressionable Hugh Hefner saw flickers of a life larger and richer than he could imagine. It was Flash Gordon's space girl paramour, the radiantly blonde Dale Arden, who stirred him first, in the thirteen-part 1936 serial *Space Soldiers*: "That was the only really sexy serial ever produced! The final scene was an open-mouth kiss!" This image would never leave his fantasies and he would look for a bit of Dale Arden in every blonde who entered his viewfinder thereafter. The irony, however, is that Dale Arden was played by a nineteen-year-old actress named Jean Rogers, a brunette who dyed her hair blonde for the role. (Not that he wouldn't have an everlasting weakness for brunettes as well, but still . . .)

*O*f Hef and Hair Tint

WHAT COLOR MEANS

Per unimpeachable experience, what are the qualities of allure specific to . . .

BRUNETTES?

There is almost a wife-and-mistress connection with brunettes and blondes. A lot of the brunettes with whom I've managed to fall in love represented not only respectability and home and marriage, but also something deeper and more romantic.

BLONDES?

What you get with blondes is something more dangerous and forbidden. There is a fascinating, universal attraction to them, representing sexuality and danger. So many blondes come out of the bottle, which is a daring choice. It's flashier and they know it.

AND WHAT ABOUT REDHEADS?

Bottle or natural, redheads are a variation of blondes for me—danger.

Understanding Their Sudden Hair Moments Can Be a Minor Art Form

When they change their hairstyle or hair color and you don't like it, don't comment on the way they look now. Just gently suggest how much you liked the way they looked before.

When She Asks "How Do I Look?"— Tread Carefully

You start with "You look perfect." Then if you don't mean it, you say "Or you might try . . ."

Expressions of Affection Never Hurt

If she lives someplace else, it's a good idea to let her know that you're thinking about her with, say, a card, an unexpected phone call, or flowers. I've always favored roses. A single long-stemmed rose can make a surprisingly amorous statement.

His gestures of love would eventually become monumental in sweep, but they began innocently enough. Summer 1944: Before shipping off for army infantry training (he would serve stateside for two years), he had pursued a romance with the girl he would marry five years later, sweet and pretty Mildred—Millie, really—Williams, a classmate he noticed only as his bright senior year at Steinmetz High waned. That summer they smooched (nothing more, not in this chaste era), and then he was gone and wearing fatigues and living in barracks, where he could devote himself— devote his heart—to pining for his girl back home. He wrote her bundles of letters—guileless and beseeching at once—from army bases here and there. As sex was still a distant reality (his own virginity remained intact until he was twenty-two, so as to conquer Millie) while it was also becoming foremost in his mind, this son of two repressed Midwestern Methodists rhapsodized thusly in one such missive: "HOW I'D LIKE TO TAKE YOU IN MY ARMS and hold you so very close to me, and kiss you, and more, a heck of a lot more! But maybe I'd best skip over this lightly or I'll have you blushin' again. Needless to say, I think about being intimate with you. Think about it a lot, right or wrong." Eventually he would know he was right to think about it, and he would tell generations to come just how right he was. Still, it all begins with the smallest gestures.

You Need to Know
That You Are Who You Are

How much a man can change for a woman depends only on the man. I think the real question is, How much should you change for a woman?

One of the great dangers in relationships is that a woman falls in love with you and you with her, and then she tries to change you. The truth is, if you haven't changed who you are by the time you are in your twenties, you aren't going to be doing much changing thereafter.

Let us keep in mind: he was the most housebound of all despots, hermetically sealed indoors, pale, working (and playing and romancing) at home like no one in history at this point, the first and foremost fully embedded man of Mansion Life. He holed up through most of the sixties in a brown and gray Gothic structure on Chicago's Gold Coast, in the most fabled of all urban domiciles, the original Playboy Mansion, 1340 North State Parkway, Valhalla, Sodom, Gomorrah, James Bond Heaven, etc. Basically, he went nowhere and had the world come to him. Then he started to make his TV show in California, and then there was Barbi on the set, and then love, and then the pallid one made some changes. Just for her. She threw him into sunshine, made him play tennis with her—on public courts!—and made him pedal bicycles with her around Los Angeles. This was not him, but it was him, giddily so. Never fond of travel, he suddenly found himself traveling the globe with her. He was smitten and traveling was part of the romantic pursuit.

One trip to Acapulco: They lay on the beach and saw people parasailing in the skies. She said, "Oh, that looks like fun!" He said, "Let's go do it!" He had never been able to swim. *Let's go do it!* She went first. He went next. He flew over water for her and landed safely, and remembered only then that he could have drowned. Just for her. "I would have gone without a life jacket if Barbi hadn't urged me to put one on." And she would recall, "I guess Hef is a little crazy when he gets into something. We were both like little kids with each other."

All of which is to say, anything is possible where love is concerned, even among the most unyielding of us.

*W*hen You Work with Them,
You Can't Not Notice Them

Sex in the workplace is here to stay, because that's where most of us spend so much of our time: Common interests in a common location make sexual communication and activity a certainty.

But a romance in the office can be a complicated affair in today's world, with accusations of sexual favoritism, harassment, or worse. So handle the personal part of your professional life with a reasonable amount of care and discretion. It is always important to make certain that you aren't misreading the signs of interest or uninterest in a coworker in matters of a romantic nature. Before a professional relationship can turn into a personal one—whether casual or serious—you need to be certain of the other party's interest. And you need to be concerned about the rules of engagement that may have been established in your company and the attitudes of your coworkers as well.

If you have properly weighed the considerations and consequences involved, there is little to be gained by considering all office-related romances out-of-bounds. Life is short and love conquers all. Or at least that's the way it should be.

Before he eschewed office life for the velvety cocoon of Mansion mooring, he fraternized most insatiably with females in his employ: "Offices are where you meet members of the opposite sex," he would say matter-of-factly. His directive in personnel matters was nondiscriminatory from the start. "Everyone was to be judged on ability," said one early human resource head. "But if I had a choice between two equally qualified people, I hired the more attractive one." *Playboy* receptionists therefore tended to be stunning. Upon hiring dusky Bobbie Arnstein, who would become his closest aide-de-camp and private secretary in the sixties, he leaned over her desk and instructed, "Don't think of me as your boss or the publisher of this magazine. Think of me as a guy looking for a date." She thought of him both ways and liked it just fine, as did he.

*W*hen She Is Jealous, Tenderly Try Telling the Truth

I have gone out of my way to minimize the downsides of jealousy through being open and honest in my relationships. Jealousies come out of the hypocrisy and lies of deception.

Then again, I get a pass that other guys don't, since women's expectations of me are different. It makes it easier because all of my cards are on the table.

RIGHT: *Another mermaid sighting in the Chicago Mansion's Underwater Bar.*

Your Heart Can in Fact Be Suddenly and Happily Split in Two

There's no question that it's possible to be in love with two women at the same time. I've been there.

Indeed, he has been there on the scale of French bedroom farce, except that rather than dashing in and out of pastel parlor doors, he would hop aboard his private black jet, the one christened the Big Bunny, shifting heart and libido between the Playboy Mansions in Chicago and Los Angeles, in each of which he had ensconced a separate and distinctly different Very Special Lady. He wryly called this adventure his Captain's Paradise, after the 1953 film *Captain's Paradise,* in which Alec Guinness steamed between the ports of Gibraltar and Tangier, in each of which he had ensconced a separate and distinctly different wife. This went on, most breathlessly, from May 1971 to February 1974, beginning with the arrival in Chicago of a new Playboy Club Bunny in training named Karen Christy: "A big-breasted, voluptuous, baby-faced blonde from Texas who had stepped right out of my erotic, pre-code Busby Berkeley Hollywood dreams from boyhood." (To wit: He saw in her traces of both his favorite platinum retro screen siren, Alice Faye, and the space minx Dale Arden—a heady and deadly Hefnerian yowsa combination.) She caught his eye instantly upon entering his world or House, and they made love on the big spinning Round Bed within several hours of meeting. "It was much more than lust at first sight," his friend and colleague John Dante would recall. "Romance was foremost on his mind. In the end, he cared about her as much as he did for any love of his life."

RIGHT: *With Karen Christy on Movie Night at the Chicago Mansion.*

Problem was: There was Barbi, for whom he did care as much as he did for any love of his life. Not only had she scouted out the property that was now the Playboy Mansion West, she was the reigning first lady of said Shangri-la. With the acquisition of his soon-to-be-legendary California estate and the ascension of Barbi three years before, he had subdivided his life, keeping tabs on his magazine and empire business in Chicago while reviving himself in the arid Western breeze, accompanied by the twinkling brunette coed who had stolen his high school retentive heart. But now, suddenly, here was this sultry, busty, and sexually playful blonde living in his own hometown Mansion, in his own hometown bedroom, with him, while Barbi roosted in his own West Coast lair, knowing nothing of what had developed in Chicago. And had continued to develop. He quickly began bestowing tokens of love, one after another, on Karen Christy, perhaps to ameliorate the fact that the world already knew of Barbi, perfectly sunny and telegenic media accoutrement that she was. Thus Karen, the sweet and easygoing country girl, received, according to legend, a diamond watch, a full-length white mink coat, a diamond Tiffany cocktail ring (for her twenty-first birthday), an emerald ring, a silver fox jacket, a painting by Matisse, a Mark IV Lincoln, and even a Persian cat. Quoth Hef: "A painting by Matisse? I think I'd remember that. It makes a good story, and someone once said if the life doesn't live up to the legend, print the legend."

For her part, she outdid herself making him feel loved:

As a self-acknowledged romantic fool, he had become fond of a pop tune called "Tie a Yellow Ribbon 'Round the Old Oak Tree"; upon his return from one lengthy Los Angeles trip, Karen had tied yellow ribbons around the branches of each tree in the Chicago Mansion front yard. He was and would continue to be a sucker for such gestures. But he would never forget that act in particular.

"I was rather crazily in love with them both," he said later. "I selfishly recognized that if I had a combination of the two of them—Barbi and Karen—I would have the perfect girlfriend. Barbi was a Jewish princess: materialistic, career-oriented, but faithful and ideally adept in social scenarios. And Karen was devoted to me, had the common interests, enjoyed playing all the board games I loved to play, and had no aspirations to a career—no aspirations other than just to be devoted to me." If he had to choose one to live on a deserted island with him, he noted, he would have chosen Karen—no public outings there, after all. But he would never live on a deserted island.

So now and then one of them would visit the other Mansion—Barbi to Chicago, Karen to California—and the business of hiding Karen's stray white bobby pins became an obsession, and whenever Barbi found a white bobby pin, it was an object of grim curiosity. And then, in the autumn of 1973, *Time* magazine photographed him in California with Barbi and in Chicago with Karen. Which revealed to Barbi that something was up. "I was, in effect, ratted out," he would say, "and everything came to a head in momentous show-downs with both of them."

Barbi left immediately. He begged her to return. She did eventually, while always thereafter maintaining an apartment of her own in Los Angeles, just in case. Karen stayed until she could no longer. She knew Barbi had returned to Mansion West, knew that his excuses and platitudes had grown thinner than air. When she left Chicago, he realized that he had no further need for Chicago life. He went back west, for the most part, and stayed there, stayed even after Barbi could wait no longer for commitment from him. And that was when she left as well, eight years following her pronouncement that she had never dated anyone over the age of twenty-four. Not that they stopped loving each other. Not that he stopped loving either one of them.

The Nevers of Love—Pay Attention

Don't make a pass at another woman while in the presence of your date. It's demeaning to you and to her as well. If a guy hit on a girl in my company, I'd say something about it. But I don't tend to have that problem. As Jimmy Caan once said, "You don't mess with the sheriff's girl."

There Is No Shame in Showing Your Tears

When a woman cries, you console her and sometimes you cry with her. The ability to keep those emotions close to the surface is a very good thing for all of us. The notion that men don't or shouldn't cry is naive. Men can and should.

A special moment with Special Lady Shannon Tweed.

Frank Sinatra could never quite fathom what Hefner had created for himself. Sinatra wooed like few others in human life, and rarely failed to get that which he wanted, female-wise, and all else–wise. But now there was this Hefner cat, with the big house in Chicago, which was Frank's kind of town, and in this big house were all these chickies, and they all loved Hefner just a little too much for Frank's taste. Frank was puzzled, but appreciated the chickies that he saw before him and those spread on Hefner's magazine pages, too. Hefner, a swell enough fellow, visited Sinatra on a movie set in Miami in 1959, and he had this fantastic broad with him named Joyce Nizzari, and Frank made a play for her, at first unbeknownst to Hefner. (Hef grew up listening to, and aspiring to, the power of Swoonatra: "His songs supplied the words and music to our dreams and yearnings. . . . Sinatra really *was* the voice of our time.")

He threw a party for Frank a few years later at the Chicago House, and Frank drew a bead on Hef's latest girl, Joni Mattis, who would later become Hef's key social secretary but was at that point simply Hef's latest girl. Frank moved in on her as well. "Actually, he hit on her *because* she *was* my girlfriend," Hefner would recall. "He was troubled, I learned later, by the fact that I had all the girls. Of course, if someone is going to try to hustle a couple of your girlfriends, it might as well be Sinatra."

The two preeminent swingers of the twentieth century engaged as such, in tender combat over female flesh, and both could only shrug when it was over.

Striking Out Is Actually Good for You

We all fail from time to time, and that's not a bad thing. There are going to be women who say no. The possibility of failure adds something to it. If every woman found you desirable, that would be pathetic. If it were a certainty, how boring life would be. It's the adventure that makes it worthwhile.

———————

It's Over When You Know
It Won't Hurt You to End It

A relationship is ready to end when those special feelings disappear and you're simply going through the motions. When the relationship no longer feeds or fuels you or the other person, but instead becomes hurtful, unpleasant, or meaningless. It isn't fair to you or the other person to go through life like that.

———————

But It's Better to Remain Friends, No Matter What

Sometimes people wind up so hurt and disillusioned at the end of a relationship that they end up hating each another. But they pay a very dear price for that. If you loved them once, there must still be qualities there that make a friendship possible. Otherwise, you are in conflict with part of your own existence.

He is remarkable in his ability to stay friends with former lovers, and inspiring as well: "I have slept with thousands of women, and they still like me," he says without a hint of braggadocio. They attest to as much: "Nobody can really let go of him," one longtime girlfriend declared. "You can hate him, hate him, hate him, but at the same time you have all these emotional mushy feelings about Hef. That's why he's still friends with all of us." Indeed, they are always welcomed back onto his grounds, as they never do leave his heart. And so you see them turn up with their children for the Mansion Easter egg hunts. You see him beam when they tell them about their new lives and new loves. He has never, in fact, actually left a relationship besides the very first one, his early marriage to Millie. Since then, they have all left him, largely because not one of them could make him hers alone. And yet even Millie, who remarried twice and successfully raised his first two children, went to work for decades in his company's personnel department, never really moved all that far from him. So, too, there is the most literal of aftermath connectives, that of the second Mrs. Hefner, Kimberley, for whom he purchased the estate adjacent to Mansion West, on the other side of a large stone wall into which a gate was set so that she and their two young sons could readily come and go. They would remain close in every meaningful way. "She probably loves me more now than she did when we were married," he said some years after she had become the Very Special Neighbor Lady, literally the Girl Next Door. This ability to remain connected is an art form all his own.

*I*f It Goes Away, It Will Come Again

The best antidote for a lost love is a new one.

We delude ourselves with the notion that somehow there is only one person out there who is a soulmate waiting for you. Emotionally, you don't fully believe that you can ever have those feelings again for someone new, that you'll ever find another comparable. That's an illusion. You can find it again because what you're really finding, by and large, is someone with common interests onto whom you can project your own needs and desires.

The reality is that life, especially in this regard, is like a movie: There are many appropriate people who can be cast in that costarring role. When you're dealing with lost love, it's time to just start the casting process all over again.

Only Fools Don't Fall Once More

Broken hearts are like broken legs. They needn't be fatal. Only a foolish person doesn't leave the heart open for the joy and pain of love again. If not, you are the loser for it. In fact, you are half alive if you are not either in love or willing to continue to have the capacity for those feelings.

Time Itself Tells the Truth

I see relationships at the time through a romantic haze. Only later on do you get some sense of what the relationship was really all about.

"We've all been there," he has said of love gone awry. "We've all had our punches in the gut." His favorite film is *Casablanca,* and he often sees himself as Rick Blaine waiting at the Paris train depot for Ilsa Lund, who never comes, reading her farewell letter in the rain, which blurs the ink. He often views himself as the guy left standing in the rain, if only temporarily. One of his secretaries once noted: "He imagined at every party that he would see a girl across a crowded room, their eyes would meet, violins would start to play, and he would feel that pit-a-pat." So it was that three days after Barbi had moved out for good, he threw himself a party stocked as ever with dozens of beautiful women. And there his eyes met those of a cherubic nineteen-year-old former Bible-school teacher named Sondra Theodore. Violins did not play, but Barry White's "Baby Blue Panties" did, and they danced to it as their first dance and made love that very night. She would soon be wearing a diamond necklace that spelled out the words *Baby Blue* and would be known for the next five years as his Special Lady. Moss, it turns out, grows only outside the Playboy Mansion.

Part 2

HEFSTYLE

The Mansion Life

And so one man created two houses and all men would forever want to go to these houses, to be inside. It began with a house in Chicago, where he too began: "I remember, in the days prior to the magazine, walking the streets of Chicago late at night, looking at the lights in the high-rise apartment buildings and very much wanting to be part of the good life I thought the people in those buildings must be leading." And so he wanted. And so he got. Eventually, that which was once considered urban good life would, in this particular Chicago house, under this particular man's sway, turn into Good Life supernova. This house, his house, of course, was the original Playboy Mansion, a stately turn-of-the-century monolith, a mere seventy rooms looming, glistening, three blocks from Lake Michigan, imposing its majesty on a leafy Gold Coast street of swells all forever to be outswelled. Six years into his empire-building, in a 1959 year-end letter to stockholders, the manor's prescient future occupant—this thirty-three-year-old workaholic editor/publisher/dreamer—wrote, almost as an afterthought: "On the personal side, we've bought a house at 1340 North State Parkway, which should make the living considerably easier and more pleasant. It is a magnificent place, with a

giant main room that will be great for parties; we're building an elaborate indoor swimming pool downstairs that will make this mansion the talk of all Chicago. It should help me get away from the office scene a bit and relax a little more."

Once he sealed himself within his grand new vacuum, work and play fused, intermingled, moved as one. Regimen knew no boundaries —a beautiful thing. Why commute? Just move the paperwork off the bed and make room for the girls. Hours were not wasted as much as savored. "Separates me from the wasted motions," he said. Also, most memorably: "The Mansion ended up working so well that going out came to seem like a useless exercise. What the hell was I supposed to go out for?" He barely went out, for certain. Maybe eight times in nine years, or so myth has it, but no one kept score, really. Once, when he and a Lady stepped outdoors during a blizzard to build a snowman in the front yard, panic seized the staff—"like there'd been a prison break," he would say, chuckling. "He's *gone out!* Hef's gone out!'"

He was never lonely therein. On a white French door that gave way to his vast ballroom—where two suits of armor stood sentry over bacchanals unending—there was affixed the most notorious brass plaque in the history of threshold passage. In Latin, it warned: *Si Non Oscillas Noli Tintinnare.* ("If you don't swing, don't ring.")

Inside, on good nights, amid the paintings of Picasso and de Kooning, amid the carved oak filigrees and the mammoth corniced pillars, jazz wailed, martinis rattled, Bunnies grooved, frugging up a storm. All such happenings took place just one flight above the indoor tropical pool, whose cave of hidden love—the Woo Grotto, it was called—was visible only to those who peeped down through a trapdoor, also hidden, in the ballroom floor. Those who swam elsewhere in the pool, meanwhile, could be viewed through a picture window in the subterranean underwater bar, most easily reached by sliding down a brass firepole. (Both

Dean Martin and Batman reportedly stole Hefner's pole notion for their respective TV shows.) Other accoutrements abounded: girls, girls, girls, of course, plus secret passages and nooks, a game room, a bowling alley, a steam room, fourth-floor Bunny dormitories (*convenience!*), red-liveried housemen, a 24-hour kitchen, spiral stairways, an electronic entertainment room (replete with early Ampex videotape recorders in the era when your basic video recorder cost twenty grand), and a hi-fi stereo console the length of a limousine with state-of-the-art features—hissless bliss. Then, too, there was his prized gold-fauceted Roman bath, which comfortably seated eight beneath a gentle spray of drizzle mists. As such, the Master of the Mansion could do, or view, whatever he wanted whenever he wanted it.

Most important, however, without question, there was the Round Rotating Bed—historic! The Bed that launched a thousand hips! The most famous bed in the annals of time! *The* Bed, period.

But we will get back to that soon enough.

$\mathcal{Y}$ou Are Where You Live

Your pad—or your crib, as it's now called—is key. It's an extension of who you are. And it's the environment in which you are going to be spending some of the best times of your life. So it should be a projection of your own personality.

The Existential Importance of Hef's House Explained

Playboy cartoon, 1970: A man has clambered to a mountain peak to beg wisdom from a cross-legged guru. Guru tells man: "In a place called Chicago . . . there's a man who lives in a mansion full of beautiful women and wears pajamas all the time. Sit at his feet and learn from him, for he has found the secret of true happiness."

Pallor—however defiant, however triumphant—will wear upon a man's soul, alas. The Great Indoors, the Pneumatic Era, the Chicago Hermitage eventually began to fatigue its chief proponent; he needed fresh air; he took flight. On the Big Bunny, his glorious jet-black DC-9, he flew west, to Los Angeles, birthplace of his formative Hollywood dreams, where show business wanted his business more than ever. He flew there and flew there until a house was found to keep him there. Paradise found: January 1971. Barbi saw it first and advised him of it; besotted by the splendor, he bought it in February. A baronial Tudor manor perched atop the greenest of slopes, set on five and a half acres of what would become his Eden—this was his Hollywood sequel: "A new Playboy Mansion for a new decade," he would say, "interconnected to nature as the Chicago Mansion could never be. I had found the place where I would live out my life, and do my best to create a heaven on earth."

Playboy Mansion West would forever be the prettier sister, the sun-drenched blonde versus the dusky brunette, appropriately curvier of terrain, and what foliage! Heaven could only hope. Here, in this soft crook of Charing Cross Road—pristine epicenter of Holmby Hills—he would design his Shangri-la from scratch, take a great barren backyard (save for Southern California's only stand of redwoods) and install an oasis, verdant and wet. Like a Midas possessed, he oversaw all minutiae: *"Where the hell are my lily pads?"* he famously inquired at one early juncture. Soon the property that had come sans pool had its own lagoon, with waterfalls spilling over a Grotto of steaming whirlpools beside koi ponds set in rolling lawns on which flamingos mingled with peacocks, cranes with ducks, a llama nibbled flowers, and—poetically—rabbits ruled. Wildlife flourished, but so too did the Wild Life, amongst and betwixt consenting adults—and this, of course, is what gave the lay of the land, if you will, its legacy.

Naturally, then, the libertine seventies found their test laboratory at Mansion West: Monkeys swung in the trees, but humans swung everywhere else. Hef had arranged the accommodations—even the Game House had mirrored love nooks. Meanwhile, his own Master Bed West, not round but extra vast, with nude nymphs carved in oak relief, with automated movable curtains and mirrors and

headboard—he would ride the box springs therein like a sultan on his magic carpet!

Still, no setting lured besporting events like the Grotto. Four Jacuzzis burbled within, so as to tenderize moments most tender, amid boulders and candlelight. "If those rocks could talk . . ." He would often muse and tantalize at once. (To finish the sentence might have finished careers.) But it is fair to say that those rocks have seen most everything and everyone (celebrity-wise) making waves, usually without clothes. Of course, there was the night of Hef's fifty-eighth birthday, on which eighteen beautiful naked women waited in his Grotto to fete him, and him alone, as speakers hidden in the rocks blared "To All the Girls I Loved Before"—the popular song that had been officially dedicated to him alone.

As he would say then and ever, "Just another typical day at the Mansion . . ."

The Mansion West Toast to Male Camaraderie

As coined for special occasions of fraternization by grateful Mansion habitué and Hef friend actor Robert Culp: "Gentlemen, gentlemen, be of good cheer, for *they* are out there, and *we* are in here!"

The Center of the World Is Where You Wake Up

For me, the most important room of the house has always been the bedroom. No surprise. It's where you do your best work and play. At the original Playboy Mansion in Chicago, I had the rotating, vibrating bed. It managed to turn each of the four sides of the room into a different living experience. The joke at the time was that it spun at 78, 33⅓, and 45 rpm like the old record players, which wasn't true. But it permitted me to separately face the television area, the fireplace, the desktop headboard, or the dining area.

The bed in Los Angeles is larger but more traditional in shape. It can easily accommodate twelve. And its special features can transform it into a little theater—with a wall-size television screen and a control panel that operates the lighting, curtains, drapes, music, and a projection system that includes videotape, DVD, laser, and satellite, cable, and regular TV. Your bed should be the center of the best part of your life.

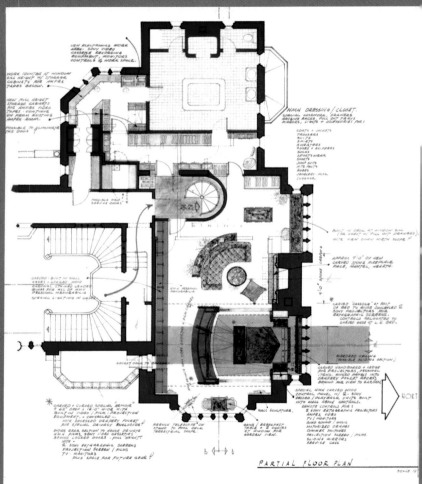

The truly best-laid plans: My Mansion West Bedroom.

Whither the Bed of all Beds? Perfectly round, eight and a half feet in diameter, its rotations made it, well, *revolutionary*—going clockwise or counterclockwise at the twist of a dial in the headboard controls, purring softly, turning, turning—the laziest susan ever! Without moving an inch, he moved his Chicago bedroom, effectively subdividing a white-carpeted universe (remove shoes, please)—sectional permissiveness! "Hef—in a James Bond world," wrote Tom Wolfe, who saw the Bed for exactly what it was: "the center of the world!"

*M*oonlight Can Become You

Working and playing all night has its advantages. I started doing it early on, before the Mansion, and learned something important about myself. I would come home at eight or nine in the morning and see people waiting to go to work, thinking how I would hate to be living that other life. I'd rather live by night and sleep during the day because all the good stuff happens at night.

He lived for whenever, especially in the Chicago Mansion. Draped out and ignored, the sun never shone in the house. Time of day meant nothing there. He liked it that way, liked to stay up for days on end, editing, philosophizing, discoursing, loving, writing memos, playing games. (Forty-hour Pepsi-fueled, Dexedrine-enhanced backgammon or Monopoly marathons! A regular occurrence!) "The wee hours were the whee hours," he said, "because while the rest of the world was asleep, romantic dreams were more likely to come true." Thus, party nights became party mornings. Norman Mailer, who observed his share of such nights, wrote of one: "The party was very big, and it was a good party. The music went all the way down into the hour or two before breakfast, but no one saw the dawn come in, because the party was at Hugh Hefner's house, which is one of the most extraordinary houses in America. I never saw the sky from that room, and so there was a timeless, spaceless sensation. . . . Timeless, spaceless, it was outward bound."

Often, at such parties, the host would never appear—he was Gatsby of Chicago in those days. Or he would appear briefly, then return to his chambers, with or without female accompaniment, to conduct the business of surveying corporate landscape and magazine layouts. He no longer went to the office; his bed was his twirling twenty-four-hour desktop, papers and printouts and color transparencies strewn everywhere. Riding the Bed in 1965, amid the clutter, he explained himself and his work habits to Tom Wolfe: "I don't take calls anymore, I just return them. I don't have any in-boxes and out-boxes. I don't have to arrange my life by other people's *hours*. I don't always have to be in some boring con-

ference. I don't have to go through business lunches and a lot of formalities. I don't even shave if I don't feel like it. I don't have to get dressed. I don't have to put on a shirt and a tie and a suit every day. I just put on a *bathrobe!*"

And what he wore under that bathrobe, of course, would become for him what a hat was for Sinatra. The signature silken ensemble—legendarily, indelibly all his own.

Pajamas Are a Playboy's Best Friend

One of the key moments of my life was the discovery that I could get away with wearing pajamas most of the time. It simplified that first decision of the day: What am I going to wear? The answer is black when I'm working during the day, and brighter colors at night. I wear them for both the comfort and the style. I have about twenty different colors, but I tend to favor purple. It has a nice kind of elegant quality and goes well with the smoking jackets, which are usually red satin or black velvet.

The first pair of pajamas I had made to order was satin. That didn't work very well because satin wrinkles and my sheets are also satin. There was a lot of sliding off the bed and pillows flying in all directions. Ever since, I've had them custom-made in silk. I wouldn't care to ever go back to cotton.

"We like our apartment," he wrote in the introduction to Volume 1, Number 1, of *Playboy* magazine, December 1953. By then, ensconced with wife, Millie, and baby daughter, Christie, he had turned an apartment in Hyde Park, at 6052 South Harper, in the shadow of the University of Chicago, into a rarefied bohemian den that boasted Hans Knoll tables and Eames chairs and grass walls and bamboo shades and a nursery wallpapered with Pogo cartoons.

"He did it all," said Millie. "He controlled every aspect of it." It became a salon for thinkers, for those rethinking their lives. He instigated talk and games and randy notions, and friends were intrigued. Said one woman, who would show up with her estranged husband (bohemian!): "Being in that apartment—the furnishings, the people and the good conversation—all of it made me feel on the cutting edge of an exciting world. I could always count on a good discussion taking place, besides the stag movies and the banned books."

Next sentence from Volume 1, Number 1 (re: "We like our apartment"): "We enjoy mixing up cocktails and an hors d'oeuvre or two, putting a little mood music on the phonograph, and inviting in a female acquaintance for a quiet discussion on Picasso, Nietzsche, jazz, sex." He wrote from real and imagined experience. He would only experience more. Meanwhile the phonograph beckons . . .

Hef's Music to Woo By

The best songs for seduction are the ones that your date responds to, and these can be as different as day and night.

Some respond to Sinatra and some like hip-hop ("Head down, ass up, that's the way we like to fuck . . ."). As in all matters of taste, you need to choose what you think your companion will find most pleasing. That may seem obvious, but many potential relationships go astray at the outset because you don't make an appropriate connection.

The list of my favorites is endless. Each song evokes a different memory, a yearning, a dream.

"**Stardust**"—Hoagy Carmichael classic, sung by almost anyone

"**As Time Goes By**"—a favorite song from my favorite movie

"**Sophisticated Lady**"—Duke Ellington

"**Dream**"—Jo Stafford and the Pied Pipers

"**Candy**"—Johnny Mercer

"**Is That All There Is?**"—Peggy Lee

"**Something Cool**"—June Christy ▶

"It's a Blue World"—Mel Torme
"One for My Baby"—Frank Sinatra
"If You Were Mine"—Billie Holiday
"It's Like Reaching for the Moon"
    —Billie Holiday
"Let's Get Lost"—Chet Baker
"Quiet Nights of Quiet Stars"
    —Astrid Gilberto
"Misty"—Errol Garner
"In the Wee Small Hours of the Morning"
    —Frank Sinatra
"It Never Entered My Mind"—Frank Sinatra
"But Not for Me"—Jackie Gleason Orchestra
    with Bobby Hackett
"Wishing"—Vera Lynn
"We'll Meet Again"—Vera Lynn
"Hold My Hand"—Al Bowlly
"Love Locked Out"—Al Bowlly
"Midnight, the Stars, and You"—Al Bowlly
"Without a Word of Warning"—Bing Crosby
"You and Me"—Peter Allen
"Everything Old Is New Again"—Peter Allen
"Can't We Be Friends?"—Frank Sinatra
"Mood Indigo"—Frank Sinatra
"I'll Be Your Friend, with Pleasure"
    —Bix Beiderbecke

Nobody will ever dance like him. Voted the best jitter-bugger in his high school class, he would remain all about slippery shuffles and twists, elbows pumping fast or slow, depending on the tune. His rhythm would always be correct, just unusual. There is video evidence aplenty—from such sixties television novelties as *Playboy's Penthouse* and *Playboy After Dark* on through a spry handful of late seventies network specials, where a nation learned that disco music had somehow overtaken it. Like no one else, he could become the most interesting Caucasian disco inferno on any floor.

*W*hen Dancing with Her and She Insists on Leading, Understand Just This

It all depends on where she wants to lead you . . .

As a boy, he had everybody come over: "Mine was the home where all the children came to play." This, too, never changed. He was born to host, never to guest. At other homes, he would be uneasy. At his own, he would exist only to welcome. His instinct was to create a nucleus of friends, of merry happenstance. Thus, the Parties. Oh, the Parties. He would perfect the art of throwing them. Over years, he would spend whatever it took just to throw them just right. As he favored sleepwear for himself, many of these parties would require just the same—lingerie especially—on New Year's Eve, and at his April ninth birthday bash, and again at the most notorious annual bacchanal occurring anywhere on the planet, the one called a Midsummer Night's Dream, which remains the lawn party of all lawn parties, as he created quite a Californian lawn for himself, and for such debauchery. It is an uninhibited lingerie-and-pajamas-only affair that is arguably the most coveted invitation in Los Angeles. "There is a pleasure to being one of the hosts that is difficult to appreciate," he would say. "Unless you're in a position where you can do it. I don't really know why it's true, but I get a great deal of extra pleasure out of sharing all of this with friends. I don't see how one *would* enjoy it if one weren't able to share it with friends."

Welcome to a Mansion Party

STAFF MEMO, HEFSTYLE

(1) THE RIGHT KIND OF ENVIRONMENT

MIDSUMMER NIGHT'S DREAM

Roman and Greek Mythology Theme Pajama Party

SATURDAY, AUGUST 3, 2002

Baskets of Lifestyles condoms out in bathhouse and on shelf in grotto at all of Hef's major events.

Decorations: A Midsummer Night's Roman and Greek Mythology Theme with Satyrs and Pans, statues, murals, flowers, twinkle lights, gold, fuchsia and red fabrics, neon palm trees, gold sequined lamé linens.

Dance Area: 24-by-28-foot lit computerized dance floor; 34 low 48-inch-round tables, with colorful pillows, gold sequined lamé linens, and low centerpieces

Stage: 8 feet by 36 feet east of dance floor

Grotto: Lots of lit candles, baby oil, towels and robes— butlers to police towels and robes and check on abundance of candles and baby oil.

(2) GOOD FOOD AND DRINK

Kitchen: Please make Jell-O shots for painted nude ladies to pass

Hors D'oeuvres: 8:00 P.M.–12:30 A.M.

Buffets: 9:00 P.M.–MIDNIGHT Pool terrace

Dessert: 10:00 P.M.–3:00 A.M. Northwest corner upper pool terrace. / 1:00 A.M.–3:00 A.M. Dining room open for coffee, cookies and cake.

(3) PLENTY OF TOILET FACILITIES

Bathrooms: Outside doors of bathhouse's bathrooms locked open. Six Porta-Potties south of pool entrance.

(4) TWO WOMEN FOR EVERY MAN

Entertainment: Nude painted dancers on platforms
   Nude painted ladies passing Jell-O shots
   Playmates/guests will also be painted.

(5) ET CETERA

Maintenance: (a) Hef wishes gate between mansion and Kimberley properties locked for all his private parties. (b) Hef has requested live ferns in grotto. (c) Toys in library and in the game house need to be put up. Remove Salvador Dalí painting in great hall and lock it away.

Animal Department: Greenhouse aviary open to tour until 10:00 P.M. Staff person to stand by animal cages and all cages locked.

Note from 1999: Only one neighbor complaint called in at 1:20 A.M. about noise from guests behind the game house. Security confirmed that one girl had just been there and was loud, close to yelling.

Successful Party Requires
Female Overpopulation

The key to a party is the right kind of environment, good food and drink, plenty of toilet facilities, and first and foremost, the crowd. The worst parties are those that have too many men hoping to get lucky. The best parties, for both sexes, have the ratio of about two to one— women to men.

Truly, he would probably prefer a seven-to-one ratio. The ramifications of the GI Bill taught him as much. Upon release from the army, on campus at the University of Illinois, he saw ratios of seven guys to one girl: "At the time, I thought, if I can control the situation in the future, I will reverse those numbers. I did my best."

The first parties were haphazard affairs. He had bought himself the Mansion in Chicago, and it was unfurnished and missing the touches of happy madness that distinguished it in the future. It was basically a big empty house. But he had started taping the black-and-white syndicated television show called *Playboy's Penthouse* (viewers rode a faux elevator up to doors that opened into Hefworld, 1959; grab a martini glass and start wandering—Ella Fitzgerald and Lenny Bruce and Nat "King" Cole will be here in a minute!), and there needed to be an after-party, a release. So ten minutes away was this home, and that is where it all began. "Those parties would start post-midnight and go to dawn," he recalls. And whatever faux party had just been taped, so as to excite the national libido, was then surpassed by an actuality in a big old empty house (Ella and Lenny and Nat will be here soon).

Once the Mansion had become legendary, and everyone from Sinatra to Streisand, from Ali to DiMaggio, from Johnny Carson to Dean Martin, began passing through the portals, there came the most notorious three-day debauch in domicile's history: The Rolling Stones came to stay during the Chicago leg of their 1972 world tour—the high point, they claimed, of that odyssey. They had, in fact, requested to come live with Hef. The week was one in which anything could—and did—happen, including an impromptu concert in the ballroom by Stevie Wonder, who had been touring as the Stones' opening act. Before it was over, after they had frolicked their way through the Bunny dormitories and shared their host's Roman bath with a bevy of Bunnies, it occurred to many that they might have actually overstayed their welcome, as the resulting staff memo would indicate.

What Happens When a Party Goes Wrong

THE ROLLING STONES
VISIT THE MANSION

6/28/72 memo from Mary O'Connor to Richard Rosenzweig

Re: Damage toll of the Rolling Stones

For your information, the following is a list of damage that resulted from the visit of the Rolling Stones:

- Red and Blue Room fixture was damaged and both glass bulb protectors had to be replaced.

- The white rug in this bathroom was burnt and needed to be replaced.

- The toilet seat was also burnt and had to be replaced.

- Two bath mats and four towels were also burnt.

- Drapes in the Red Room were pulled down on one side and the traverse rod had to be replaced.

- Red Room chair and couch are stained, possibly to the point of needing reupholstering.

- Red Room bedspread is badly stained. We are hoping it will come out in cleaning.

- Blue Room bedspread was not only stained, but also full of cigarette burns.

- Four sheets and two pillowcases were taken from the beds in the Blue Room.

- Brown Room and Gold Room velvet bedspreads were all very badly stained. We do not know yet whether the cleaners were able to do anything about this.

In addition to this, miscellaneous articles including razor blades were allowed to go down the drain in the Gold Room sink, rendering that room unusable for several days, and caused us to go into the wall to clear the pipes.

He picked his preferred poison as a boy and never abandoned it. He is a Pepsi man. Actually, he is a Pepsi Generation unto himself. Famously, through the sixties, he was photographed swigging from Pepsi bottles; butlers in his homes were always instructed to provide a new bottle if they saw one half empty. Or if he was seen without a Pepsi in his hand, they were to immediately fill that hand with a

Pepsi bottle. He would drain three dozen bottles a day, caffeinating himself royally. In 1962, it was reported that his annual Pepsi consumption equaled that of a small African country. There was a time when Coca-Cola was all but banned from his premises, but his soft-drink bias softened eventually, since his brother, Keith, was not a Pepsi man. (As far as he remembers, Hef chose Pepsi over Coke although it was "twice as much for a nickel too," when he was young.) But at parties, then and now, if he holds a glass that would seem to contain Pepsi on the rocks, the drink almost certainly also contains Jack Daniel's—"My Pal Jack," he calls it. And at such parties, if he is seen without a full glass in his hand, butlers will place a new full glass in his hand. It is what they do.

---

*D*rink Like Hef

A COCKTAIL ANATOMY—"MY PAL JACK"

As explained by Mansion mixologist William Lipsher, aka Willie the Bartender

Just as he's done with his closest friends, Hef has stuck by (and also with) Jack Daniel's and cola for a long, long time. He is never overindulgent; one or two drinks a night will suffice.

▶

His drink is always served in what the butlers call an HMH glass (a 10-ounce clear, dimpled tumbler). Several HMH glasses are always kept in a cupboard in the pantry. Everyone else's drinks are served in sturdier, longer-lasting glassware.

When parties are poolside, everyone's beverages are served in plastic (for safety). Everyone's but Hef's, of course. It's his house. He can take his HMH glass wherever he wants.

When he approaches the bar for his drink, I'll fill the HMH glass with ice (I always make sure the little cubes are jingling loose; icebergs are not cool); then, using a shot glass, I'll pour on exactly one ounce of Jack. That's the official amount he wants per drink. I'll top it off with Pepsi and, using a retro-style Playboy bunny stir stick, proudly mix the contents with a flourish and a smile.

As a beginning bartender I learned to leave a quarter inch of space at the top of each drink. Looks great. Less spilling. Early on in my Playboy days, though, that quarter inch was too much space for my boss's tastes. He requested more Pepsi. Who was I to argue? So while everyone else's drink still gets that quarter inch of graphically aesthetic space, I'll top off Hef's that extra eighth inch, because that's the way he wants it.

I complete the routine by placing a napkin on the bar before him, setting his drink on it, and wishing him "Cheers."

He will always be remembered with the pipe. He would clench it, fidget with it, speak through it, wave it emphatically, even smoke it. He took it up mostly as a television prop ("I thought it looked cool"), and thereafter it would be difficult to think of him without it. Thus, one of the most legendary oral fixations in history was born. After suffering a minor stroke in 1985—from which he began to recover within two weeks—he put his pipes away for good and never missed them. Still, at certain Halloween parties, he has been known to come dressed as Hugh Hefner. When he does that, he fishes out one of his old numbers and moves about the property making like himself from thirty years before—the prototype of retro cool, to be sure.

The Best Accessory: Taking Up the Pipe

The inspiration for the pipe came from the pop culture of my childhood. Pat Ryan in the Terry *and the* Pirates *comic strip smoked a pipe, and he was a dashing fellow, always on top of his game. Sherlock Holmes—one of my early heroes—also was a pipe smoker and spent a lot of time in his bathrobe. There may be some subconscious connection there. But when I started smoking the pipe in the late fifties, it was more for style than anything else. It was something to do with my hands. When I was hosting* Playboy's Penthouse *on television, it was a nice little prop.*

Wheels Do Make a Statement

The first car that I bought for myself after I started Playboy *was a Cadillac Eldorado convertible. It was about half a block long and metallic bronze, with big fins and black leather upholstery. That was a good car. But my favorite car was my white 1959 Mercedes-Benz 300SL convertible, which I reacquired not long ago. That was the most fun I ever had behind a steering wheel.*

From the start, his magazine celebrated Materialism, the acquisition of the Good Life and all the new and shiny trap-

pings. It took him a while, however, to catch up with his credo. In December 1953, shortly after the first issue was published, the secondhand, beat-up Chevrolet coupe he had been driving went dead on him for good. He replaced it with a sturdy Raymond Loewy–designed Studebaker, which served mostly as a sensible family car. By 1955, however, once the company was flush with success, he opted one day to walk into a Cadillac showroom, collar open, looking unimpressive, feeling self-impressed. "How much does an Eldorado cost?" he asked a bored salesman who was reluctant to even hand over a brocure to him. "About sixty-five hundred," he was told. "How long would it take to get one in bronze?" he asked. A couple of weeks, he was told. "Okay, here's a check for a thousand as a down payment," he said. "When you deliver the car, I'll give you another check for the rest." He walked off with a swagger in his step. He'd never done anything like that before. He would start getting used to it.

The Big Bunny:
So You Buy a Private Jet and Paint It Black . . .

If you buy a private plane, first and foremost, you should have a bed installed. The Big Bunny was like a flying apartment. The bed had its own seat belt so you didn't have to get up during landing. It also had a shower, which was nice. Another special touch was the dance floor in the living room. Whenever there was turbulence, you were suddenly developing a new step.

When I purchased the Playboy plane, I decided to paint it black. No one had ever done that before, and some suggested that it would overheat and be difficult to see in the sky at night, but it became the most famous private jet in the world. It was a stretched version of a McDonnell Douglas DC-9. With additional fuel tanks, it had worldwide capability. The stewardesses were Jet Bunnies and they looked as though they had just stepped out of a James Bond movie. When anyone asks me if I ever miss the plane, I reply, "Only when I fly." With the Big Bunny, getting there really was half the fun.

He never traveled very easily—commercial flights were not his thrill so he eventually made sure that he would travel very well. His sleek black airship sliced through the skies for nearly six years, beginning February 1970, winging mostly between private terminals at O'Hare and Los Angeles International, between Mansions and Special Ladies. Of all the toys he had given himself, this was the biggest and arguably the best—his greatest extravagance, price tag $5.5 million, an unrivaled symbol of sybaritic engorgement. Whenever it landed, crowds gathered. The white rabbit head on the tail announced who had come to town. (Sometimes this could be deceptive, as the plane was occasionally leased to the likes of Elvis Presley and Sonny and Cher.) More flying Mansion than flying apartment, it was a plane that would normally seat more than a hundred passengers; he retrofit it

so that capacity would top out at thirty-eight and comfortably sleep twelve. It was all about more legroom for much better-looking legs. Parties swung above clouds. The Jet Bunnies were trained to cook his favorite meals at his midair whim. Movies were shown in wide-screen Cinemascope. His private quarters had a separate rear entrance, their own electronic entertainment system, and their own shower; bedcovers were silk and Tasmanian opossum fur and well romped upon. "When we went to Europe," Barbi Benton would recall, "we'd immediately go to the back of the plane, hop in the Round Bed, go to sleep, and wake up in Italy."

If there was a mother of all Big Bunny jaunts, it was the aforementioned one: Beginning in late July 1970, he and Barbi and an entourage of friends, including artist LeRoy Neiman and film critic Gene Siskel (in his universe, there would always be an entourage of friends), embarked on the most elaborate excursion of his life. Over seven and a half weeks, they flew to England and Spain, Kenya and Tanzania, Greece and Italy, Germany and France—Morocco, even, where some sultan threw them a carpeted beach party and fed them dessert laced with opiate! By 1976, however, he tired of traveling, was hardly flying to Chicago at all, and decided to sell his black bird to Venezuela Airlines for $4.2 million. The Venezuelans promptly gutted it and transformed it into a commercial carrier whose passengers would never know they rode where Hugh Hefner had slept and played and indulged in great amounts of turbulent intercourse.

*I*nsight from the President—
and a Member—of the Mile-High Club

*The reality is that having sex above the clouds is exactly
the same as having sex anywhere else. It's just a memory.
A fond memory, however.*

Part 3

THE GREAT INDOORS

*Hef's World of Film, Food,
and Adult Games*

He has starred in the Movie of his Own Life. Some time during boyhood he convinced himself that he would Do Large Things, at which point it was as though he almost believed a camera was trained upon his every ingenious move thereafter. At his famous Mansion parties, most certainly, corporate video crews follow him everywhere, recording each moment of his presence as host, while he greets guests and nuzzles women and dances into the night. He once said, "If you don't have a picture of it, how do you know it ever happened?"

To wit: He was a born visual enthusiast nonpareil—and look at where that got him. As a teen, he wrote, directed, and starred in a short film called *The Return from the Dead*, silent and faux Gothic, shot in his basement; he played a mad scientist who in his death throes is seen scrawling the words *The End* in his own blood on the floor. Love of the movies had by then seized him with ferocity. He was just eight when he saw *Tarzan and His Mate*, and his life would instantly change forever. Jane, as played by Maureen O'Sullivan, actually swam nude right in front of his impressionable eyes! "My interest in censorship came from the movies," he would later say.

Who are these men making time with bombshell Jayne Mansfield?

Indeed, he was all but entirely molded and shaped by that which he had seen in dark theaters: Precode bombshells Jean Harlow and Alice Faye fueled a lifelong lust for like bombshells. Urbane swells like Cary Grant and William Powell and Fred Astaire taught him how to be a romantic leading man, a role he would essay in new ways for other generations. Bogie showed him that being a bit of the wry rogue would never hurt, either. And then there was Marilyn Monroe, whom he first glimpsed in a trifle called *Scudda Hoo! Scudda Hey!*—her unspectacular film debut—at a theater in Danville, Illinois. He had brought Millie Williams to Danville on that June 1948 weekend so as to lose his, and her, virginity. They saw the movie the next afternoon. "You can imagine how I cherish the symbolism of that," he would say, as he is one who tends to cherish symbolism of any sort. "More than anyone else in our lifetime, Marilyn made nudity socially acceptable." Five years later, he would acquire nude calendar photos of her and make her his first cover girl and centerfold pinup, begetting all else to follow. Further symbolism: When he departs the mortal coil, he will sleep with Marilyn forever, in the drawer adjacent to hers at the Westwood Memorial mausoleum. He made sure of that.

*T*hink Cinematically

and You'll Find a Happy Ending

I've always thought about my life like a movie. You need the drama. If you think of your life that way, you get through the tough times.

———————

Mansion Movie Nights became ritual starting in Chicago. Sunday evenings he would dress casual, go share the buffet, have a few drinks, and meet Bunnies on their night off. Friends and visiting celebrities were invited to see first-run 35-millimeter showings of the latest box-office hits, projected on a large screen lowered into the ballroom,

where suits of armor flanked the portals. At Mansion West, the Sunday ritual endured, but in later years he would expand the playbill by running classic films on Monday (Manly Night, when his cronies would choose the feature du jour from the vast house collection); on Friday, for an astute group of buffs christened the Casablanca Club (Hef personally prepares insightful notes explaining the production nuances of whatever film he elects to show); and on Saturday. Like a ringleader, he wanders about his home to gather guests just before the seven o'clock (ever punctual) screening; "It's mooovie time," he will intone. When the lights dim in the Living Room—where butlers have laid out bowls of fresh popcorn and candies—he will sit on the far left end of a long leather sofa in front of the screen, and his Lady and/or Ladies will snuggle beside him. He is happiest at such times, bathed in the flickering light, watching dreams unfold. Always was.

Classic Mansion Movie Nights

HEF'S FAVORITE FILMS

Casablanca *is my favorite film for many reasons. It has everything—lost love, redemption, friendship, patriotism, humor, adventure, and a great musical score. Humphrey Bogart is my favorite actor and this is his best role, the one that made him a star.*

Then, in no special order:

- The Maltese Falcon (*another Bogart classic*)
- To Have and Have Not (*Bogart meets Bacall*)
- Singin' in the Rain (*my favorite musical*)
- City Lights (*my favorite Chaplin*)
- King Kong (*let's hear it for the big guy*)
- The Godfather I and II (*a sequel that actually makes the first film better*)
- Dr. No (*Sean Connery as Bond and Ursula Andress as the ultimate Bond Girl*)
- Goldfinger
- A Place in the Sun (*Elizabeth Taylor at her most beautiful*)
- Adam's Rib (*Tracy and Hepburn at their best*)
- Gilda (*Rita Hayworth at her best*)
- Laura (*Gene Tierney ditto*)
- The Awful Truth (*Cary Grant unforgettably funny*)
- Some Like It Hot (*Marilyn at her best*)
- Chinatown (*the best mystery since* The Maltese Falcon)

- Body Heat (*a sexy film noir mystery*)
- Raiders of the Lost Ark
- Shane (*my favorite Western*)
- *Anything with Fred Astaire and Ginger Rogers from the 1930s*
- *The best of Woody Allen, including* Annie Hall, Manhattan, Radio Days, *and* Bullets over Broadway

His Holmby Hills neighbors of yore had been heroes of his youth—Harlow, Disney (another Chicago-born dream merchant made good), Bogie and Bacall. Once asked why he didn't spend more time hobnobbing with the swells of Europe, he replied, "No, I'm more attracted to America's nobility—the kings and queens of Hollywood." Ghosts of Old Hollywood, most appropriately, seem to hover about his splendid grounds: "It has been suggested, and it's probably true, that the lifestyle here at the house, the parties et cetera, are closer to the real, *and imagined*, Old Hollywood than can be found anyplace outside of here today. In fact, the good times here now are *better*." New Hollywood, meanwhile, began prowling his premises from the moment he took up residency. In the seventies, Nicholson and Beatty and Tony Curtis and Jimmy Caan all but lived there. "They all came by because the chicks were here," the Man of the Manor has noted. Future generations would follow suit—from DiCaprio to Clooney to Maguire.

Playboy After Dark

- Casablanca—*When Bogart says to Ingrid Bergman, "Here's looking at you, kid."*
- To Have and Have Not—*When Lauren Bacall says to Bogie, "All you have to do is whistle. You know how to whistle, don't you? Just put your lips together and blow."*
- City Lights—*When the blind flower girl recovers her sight and realizes that Charlie Chaplin is her benefactor and a tramp. It is for me the most intensely moving moment in the entire history of motion pictures.*
- Now, Voyager—*Paul Henreid lighting two cigarettes and handing one to Bette Davis at the end of the film.*
- Love Affair *and* An Affair to Remember—*When Charles Boyer (and Cary Grant, in the remake) realizes that Irene Dunne (Deborah Kerr) failed to meet him at the top of the Empire State Building because she was hit by a car and is crippled.*
- King Kong—*When the big guy starts to undress Fay Wray, removing garments like petals from a flower, and when he puts her down before falling from the top of the Empire State Building. As Robert Armstrong observes, "It wasn't the planes. It was beauty killed the beast."*

Food has been as essential to Movie Nights as the movie itself. When one enters the realm of Dionysus, one expects (correctly) to feast. Dionysus, in this case, however, will eat nothing himself and only watch his guests gorge from the dining room groaning board. He will sit at the head of the table and hold court and drink his Jack and Pepsi, but never eat. He has long preferred to dine in bed, with Ladies, late at night. Moreover, the food in his buffet line would not suit him anyway. Food is an unusual area of predilection in his world.

As with most all else in his life, degustation is a steadfast ritual of quirk, truly remarkable in its precision. His is a palate both simple and, well, desperately *particular*. No mere meat-and-potatoes man, he is a meat-and-potatoes man who must have everything just so, including the arrangement of the vegetables on the plate and the location of salt and pepper shakers on the bed tray. And that is just the beginning of it. There can be no surprises, no new twists or seasonings in any time-honored recipe. Indeed, experimentation has forever been out of the question.

Getting it Just So for him is the utmost directive in the Mansion kitchen: "Hef's the easiest man in the world to please," his longtime executive assistant Mary O'Connor has said, "providing everything is done just the way he wants it." A meticulous kitchen log has always been kept in the butler's pantry describing the preparations of his meals in minute detail, with photographs of how each individual favorite meal must be presented to him. When he calls the kitchen to place his order—his summons comes as a buzz that sounds like no other sent from the property—all current activity therein stops entirely (that is to say, the preparation of the food orders of his houseguests), while staff scrambles to accommodate his cravings. Further quirks and tastes: He remains most fond of Wonder Bread, but only slices pulled from fresh unopened packs. He is also fond of pot roast, meat loaf, Lipton's chicken soup (the instant kind), and lamb chops, quite especially. Seafood does not really exist in his life. Breakfast food (eggs and bacon and hash browns and french toast, and so forth), on the other hand, is his thrill. And, more often than not, he will insist upon washing it all down with ice-cold milk in a freshly chilled highball glass. Shaken, not stirred.

And then there is the topic of fried chicken. Fried chicken has long been sacrosanct in Hefworld, and here is why: When he was a boy, his family would often go out to dinner on Sundays to a neighborhood restaurant that offered what he considered to be perfect fried chicken. He yearned for this perfect fried chicken ever after, Sundays especially. Once he became king of a Mansion, wherein he drafted memos like no others in history, he drafted this one, circa early sixties, to his kitchen staff: "This is just a note to tell you that the chicken we had over the weekend was absolutely the best I have ever had at the house. It had the dark crust on the outside, and the very tender, well-cooked

meat inside, and it was just delicious. The gravy for it still isn't all that it ought to be—not really enough meat flavor to it, not quite thick enough, and not quite creamy enough. It had a rather orange color to it, whereas my favorite fried chicken and pork chop gravy is fairly thick tan to light brown in color."

All else in his life would be gravy, if only the metaphorical kind, but still: It should be noted, by the way, that two chickens must die in order for him to be served his requisite three drumsticks per meal. He always thought well of Colonel Sanders's Kentucky Fried Chicken, with its secret herbs and spices, but even he could not wrest away that recipe. And so, when he and Barbi and contingent flew around Europe—and he refused to eat fancy food, and all else were thrilled with fancy food—his valet quietly infiltrated the haute kitchen of Maxim's in Paris, in order to instruct its chef on the art of preparing southern fried chicken, à la Hefner. ("I am pretty horny for some fried chicken," he had by then been muttering for weeks.) That night, it was unveiled to him under a silver chafing dish, along with mashed potatoes, gravy, and peas. After he consumed it, washing it down with a goblet of cold milk, the chef approached to inquire how he had liked the meal. "I've had better," said the American Playboy. The chef could only shrug and return to the kitchen, bemused and dejected at once. "I was sure," one witness recalled, "that he was going in there to blow his brains out."

Eat Like Hef

Hugh Hefner's Fried Chicken

FRESH CHICKEN PARTS
- 2 split chicken breasts
- 2 chicken thighs
- 6 chicken drumsticks

SEASONED FLOUR
- 3 cups all-purpose flour
- 1½ tablespoons Lawry's seasoned salt
- ½ teaspoon ground black pepper
- ½ teaspoon fine sea salt
- 1 tablespoon Spanish paprika
- 1½ cups Wesson oil

Preheat an electric skillet to 375°. Rinse the chicken pieces thoroughly in cold running water. Combine the flour and the seasonings. Pour the Wesson oil into the skillet. Let the oil heat up. Test by sprinkling some flour in the pan. If it bubbles, it is hot enough to start frying the chicken.

Fully dredge the wet chicken in the flour mixture and place in the skillet. Reserve the seasoned flour. Cover and allow to steam/fry for 15 minutes. Uncover and sprinkle a small amount of seasoned flour over the top of all the chicken pieces. Chicken should be a nice golden brown before

▶

turning (approximately 25 minutes). Brown the other side (approximately 15–20 minutes). Remove the chicken pieces from the skillet. Place on paper towels to drain. Set aside and keep warm. Turn off the skillet.

NOTE: When ordering the chicken parts from the butcher, all products should be specified as follows: drumsticks should weigh 2.8 to 3 ounces, thighs should weigh 3.5 to 4 ounces. and breasts should weigh 22 to 25 ounces.

Never had he actually disliked the out-of-doors. He moved west, after all, to prove as much. In fact, he would immediately become the most ardent guide for tours of the property—proudly, gleefully, goofily even—leading visitors across rolling lawns, up hill and down glade, into the tropical aquatic aviary (rare fish! rare birds! unpleasant reptiles!), into the steamy Grotto ("if only those rocks could talk . . ."), off to the squirrel monkey cages, where he'd pass green grapes through the screens into tiny simian paws. Such tours, too, would inevitably halt beyond the wishing well and the pet cemetery, linger in a lush shady copse which is the site of the great Game House, the place where he has engaged in combat more ferocious than in any executive boardroom. Here, over pool and foosball tables, in front of pinball machines (wired for free play) and electronic contraptions that screech and pulsate, he has unleashed his inner guerrilla, his secret kamikaze. If he is famously the most primal of men in his bedroom, he is even more so inside this place. Here he has fulminated, simmered, combusted, kvelled, spun, keened, twisted, hollered, wailed, swaggered, bounced, fumed, waltzed, mourned, revivified, leapt, muttered, sang, bragged, jitterbugged, fell apart, and pounded fists of anguish or pumped fists of triumph. Upon victory, he is never subtle; it is no coincidence that a replica of his star from the Hollywood Boulevard Walk of Fame was embedded in the concrete path that leads directly into his Game House.

Game Playing Gives You
Something Else to Think About

It's a great escape. That's all it is. Working hard and play-ing hard has always been what my life has been about. Particularly if you're doing things you really enjoy. When I first published Playboy, *outdoor adventure magazines for men were very popular. But as I wrote in the introduction to that initial issue, I was a little more interested in the great indoors. Apparently, I wasn't the only one. Indoors is where my favorite games are played.*

When You've Got the Hand, Protect It

It's certainly true that we went through periods of obsession in the Game Room, especially related to individual pin-ball and electronic games. Shannon Tweed, my girlfriend in the early 1980s, talks about the fact that she and the other girls viewed themselves as Pacman widows because they would sit there for hours waiting for us to get through these games. I played Pacman so obsessively that I got bursitis—like a tennis elbow for the thumb—and had to start wearing a glove during the games.

And so the greatest Playboy of them all played Games in a manner few other mortals dared to attempt or cared to imagine. It was part of showing them the way, of demonstrating that the simplest, most innocent pleasures could be indulged with a great hedonist's abandon. Even if it happened during card nights of bridge and gin and (strip?) poker, or on the slick surface of Risk and Monopoly boards, or if it required well-thumbed Scrabble and backgammon tiles—he would and did find a way to do it larger, and with epic endurance. His credo from the get-go: "Americans knew very well how to earn money, but didn't know very well how to enjoy it."

Playmates Sondra Theodore and Monique St. Pierre
watching the Playboy wizard in action.

So he decided that he would embody the fever pitch of how money and the silliest little games, the board ones, could be enjoyed. And like no pinball wizard before him, he put the joy in joystick. "This Is Real Life," he once exclaimed during an intense session captured by a documentary crew. "The rest is a game." Like no man who had ever scored with more women, he would have plaques affixed above every throbbing, humming, thumping electronic game to identify the highest scorers so far. (Inevitably, that was usually him.) Still, ever the fair-minded Midwestern boy, whenever he broke new records while playing alone (practice, practice!), he would always summon a member of his security staff to witness what he had accomplished before the new number was memorialized on a plaque. Which it would be, most immediately. For he had what, goddammit, gone and scored again? And he was playing what, fair? He said so. Midwestern integrity.

How to Win It All at Monopoly

To win consistently, you should know that the orange properties are the most valuable. You can't win with the Baltic and the Mediterranean; you can with most of the others. But it's the orange that is most valuable—it's a middle ground between the high-priced Boardwalk and the lower-priced properties. Mathematically, orange will usually prevail.

Monopoly, like Hef, was created during the Depression to give Americans big dreams to ponder, dreams that weren't yet exactly within one's grasp—kind of like the Life Philosophy that imbued him. Naturally, he played this game with insight. He also played it maniacally—the forty-hour marathons (Pepsi, Dexie, Pepsi, Dexie, Pepsi, Dexie, you get the picture) that would later be replaced only by forty-hour backgammon marathons.

Monopoly, though: cartoon capitalism and dice and play money, with play money whose bills bore his likeness where Mr. Monopoly's face used to be, with pictures of both Mansions emblazoned on the back, eventually with even an Atlantic City Playboy Casino Hotel figurine to place on the Boardwalk (like in life, in that very moment)—a personal personalized game for the Luckiest Monopolist of One Culture's Craziest Yearnings. This was the official game of the Chicago Mansion, circa early seventies, with blonde, buxom Special Lady on the side, Karen Christy, presiding. She surprised him with game tokens molded and hand-painted to represent the core players—as seen here, from left—longtime friend John Dante, secretary Bobbie Arnstein, Karen herself, Hef himself, poet/artist/contributor in residence Shel Silverstein, and fledging *Chicago Tribune* film critic Gene Siskel, whom Hef persuaded during one such faux real estate contest into becoming a film critic rather than just one more beat reporter; they shared a love of film, it turned out—who knew?

He moved the game west eventually—it was the one game that allowed him pause for conversation, which he enjoyed—and after Karen had gone, and Barbi, too, new likenesses were molded for Californians in the mix, including

one for new Special Lady Sondra Theodore, who saw her man differently during these matches: "He was great with games and fun with games. That's when his personality really came out. The tension of real life flew out of him. He relaxed. Those were the times I found that I wanted to reach out and hug him, because he's just so wonderful and witty and funny and loving—and it all came out when you sat down and played a game with Hef."

The Tao of Backgammon and Its Cunning Secrets

Of all the games we play, the one I most enjoy and that I'm best at is backgammon. It's a natural game for me and I was fortunate enough to learn from world-class players. It's all a combination of skill and luck. But more than anything, it is a running and blocking game.

And understanding the blocking portion of it is the most sophisticated form of strategy. Many players get their pieces out of play by moving them around and into their own home prematurely. The key is blocking. Of course, the other half of the game is the cube. The cube is the betting device, which makes the game particularly exciting. Knowing when to accept—or give—a double is really as important as the game itself.

There would be no meaningful conversation during backgammon—just fine, acrid, sparkling bluster. With this pursuit, his mind was buried deep into the argyle board, into the game, like with Pacman but without the *bloop* sounds. He loved the utter gentlemanly brutality of it: brain matter aswirl, hands flying, neurons snapping, and yet the constant movement, of fingers and of ego, the unending back-and-forth brag, of studious guesswork. Barbi, who had the sweetest noggin to date, who was damned good at it, who had tourneys named for her, claimed they discovered the game maybe in Africa, on the big tour of the world? "Actually," she said, "Hef was responsible for bringing backgammon to this country." He, of course, had been puzzling about it, knew about it, was waiting for it, learned it enough, then had decided in fact that Los Angeles needed a backgammon discotheque as the seventies dawned, and he opened a club minus Bunnies (not that the waitresses weren't spectacular) called Pip's, where he hunched over his game board. He and this game would never part, as he even now pulls down a board and marches it poolside to make trouble every warm summer Sunday. Near the nude sunbathers, but of course.

Part 4
THE BUSINESS OF LIFE

Dreams and the World

Here then was a young fellow (twenty-seven years old!) with an idea, a dream, an impossible dream, inculcated in him, defining him, eating him alive, with nothing else to do but just to go do it, to go make it happen. Also, and this is important, he had no money with which to do it. (He bleared his eyes at jobs that mattered not at all—promotional copy-writing! *please!*—that drove him mad, while he dreamed dreams of elsewhere.) So he borrowed against his furniture, for God's sakes! That gave him six hundred bucks, to begin with. He culled a few grand more from friends, from acquaintances, from his own folks (nice and most puzzled folks who could not bear to think of what their boy was about to do), by way of goodwill, of sheer force of will, because his eyes burned with this dream. People had to believe, had no other choice if they paid attention, and those that did became rich. (He was always one to share his bounty.) "If a guy didn't dream impossible dreams, life would hardly be worth living," he depicted himself declaring in his private cartoon-paneled autobiography, illustrating the moment of *Playboy*'s birth (the personal cartooning did not end after high school, you see). Then he had his cartoon self add, "Especially because—sometimes—even the most impossible ones come true!"

And at that moment, he had no idea of what was truly to come.

*F*ollow the Brightest Light You See in the Dark

When I was a boy growing up on the far West Side of Chicago, the beacon from the tallest skyscraper on Lake Shore Drive used to sweep across the sky at night. There was something mysterious and mystical about that beacon. It represented a world of sophistication and adventure that I could only dream about. That beacon was like the green light at the end of Daisy's dock in The Great Gatsby. *The connections between F. Scott Fitzgerald, Gatsby, and my own young dreams were powerful ones. I wanted to live in that world and chronicle it as Fitzgerald had done the roaring twenties.*

And of course that's exactly what I did. Later I even acquired the skyscraper with the beacon. It became the Playboy Building. And that beacon? It became the Bunny Beacon.

His would be a true-blue American story—a great one as well, Horatio Alger style (with sex, but still . . .)—because he quested, because he risked, because his gut told him secrets and he listened to his gut, as all humans should but all too rarely do. He was a straight arrow, born of kindly and repressed parentage, Glenn and Grace Hefner, good Methodists, simple folk and proud of it, thank you, who asked for little, who made a boy who asked for a little more. (Lights in the sky!)

The Calling

I came to a moment in time in which I realized that I did not simply want to become my parents. I did not want to simply become what someone else expected me to be. I wanted to march to a different drummer. Each of us in our own way has to find some reasonable accommodation to what other people expect of us. But first and foremost, if you don't pursue your own dreams and become the person you want to be, it's over in much too short a time.

———————

And so, married too soon, bogged down, boggled with his lot, he rolled up his sleeves, sat down at a card table, stared at his L. C. Smith typewriter, and started spinning a yarn, a concoction of bluster and hope that would become pure fortune. He had wanted to call his magazine *Stag Party,* with a logo that featured an antlered buck swilling a cocktail, which would have been most unfortunate. More fortunately a magazine called *Stag* sent him a cease-and-desist order (no antlers allowed), and then he reconsidered and found his rabbit, the ever thumping, ever procreating playboy of the animal kingdom. What would come of it, besides the best-selling men's magazine in the history of the world, in no particular order: nightclubs and hotels and casinos and resorts and women dressed as bunnies and women dressed not at all and various publications and a book imprint and merchandise bearing rabbit heads and television programs and movie productions and cable channels and video marketing and a record label and video games and a humming Website and Mansions, but certainly, and most important of all, good life, always good life, no matter what.

And so he also said: "Society may urge you to live your life for somebody else. But enlightened self-interest is for the good of everybody. If you don't care about yourself, you're going to find it difficult to care for other people. H. L. Mencken was the one who said: 'A puritan is somebody who is very upset because someone, somewhere, is having a good time.'"

The Wisdom of the White Lie

I had two different letterheads—one for Stag Party *and the other for my imaginary distributing company called Nationwide News Company. When I wrote a letter on the magazine's stationery, I was the editor, publisher, or promotion, advertising, or circulation director as circumstances dictated. When I was writing to newsdealers, I was the general manager or president of Nationwide News Company. I was the entire staff of both. That's all there was—just me, my typewriter, and that card table.*

"I wanted a job that I could love," he said. So he created one for himself, one that nobody else could ever have. He had no dough, no real experience at what he would need to do. He just let his head rumble, when he wasn't knocking it against walls: "Sometimes I would find myself in a crowded elevator or a building lobby, and I would be overwhelmed and demoralized by the notion that I was the only one who was still unplugged and disconnected." He would not be the first or the last one to feel such demoralization. And yet he had nothing to lose by sticking his long neck out. So he did.

If You Don't Reach for the Sky, You'll Never Leave the Ground Floor

You have to calculate the odds before taking risks. But if you don't take chances on the things you really want, then you'll never know. Rational risk is part of what life is all about. A man's reach should exceed his grasp, else what's a heaven for?

As a boy, he let a girl turn him inside out. As a man, he turned himself inside out. Girls, this time, would come later. "When you talk about self-reinvention," he said, "the extent to which I have done it and chronicled it—done it at a conscious level—is probably the most unique and remarkable thing about my life." He decided he was not the guy living the life he was living—married, working for people he did not want to work for, bottled up, lost as lost gets—and incited a personal rebellion. He reinvented himself, and soon enough he got the girl and the girl and the girl and the girl, et cetera.

Did we say that he got the girl?

Et cetera.

The Importance of Self-Reinvention

I'm a dreamer, a crusader who wanted to change the world. There are so many things in life that force you into a box and force you to conform to values handed down by others. When you are very young, both society and family define you. There should be a time when you begin to define yourself for yourself.

———————

*H*ef's Five Lucky Breaks

When a fellow knows that he is up to something, he might well write himself an annual letter explaining exactly what had happened during said year, for the sake of history. Here is the awestruck letter Hugh M. Hefner wrote to himself upon finishing the year in which he made a new magazine for himself, a magazine called *Playboy*.

January 1954

What do you say when a dream comes true? What words do you use? How can a guy possibly express a thing like this?

I own a magazine—a magazine of my very own. Or more precisely, I am president of, and hold a majority of the stock in, a corporation that owns a magazine. Of course, we've very little money in the bank and the road ahead will be a rough one, but nevertheless, the dream has become a reality—and whether we succeed or fail in the months and years ahead, I'm getting my chance to try.

Only a series of very lucky breaks has made this fantastic thing possible. If I believed in Fate, I'd think there was some sort of predestination in it. Certainly much of my life, and especially the last three or four years, has been a preparation for this. For there is nothing on earth I would rather be doing than editing and publishing this magazine called Playboy . . .

Lucky break #1. *We needed a gimmick. Something special for the first issue to talk about in my promotion letter to* newsdealers and attract attention to the magazine from the very start. We got a gimmick—the biggest one of the decade. The nude calendar of Marilyn Monroe had received unprecedented publicity all over the country, yet no magazine had published it calendar-size or in color. *Life* had reproduced one of the two poses in an inch-high two-color picture, and that was that. The calendar company that owned the better of the two shots (the one *Life* hadn't reproduced) was located in a Chicago suburb. I walked in there cold and came out with permission to reproduce the picture in full color for $500—and they threw in the color separations on the deal, which are worth around $400 by themselves. We'll never know how many thousands of dollars that picture was worth to us. It immediately classed us as big-time with the newsdealers and probably with our readers too.

Lucky break #2. With orders for 70,000 copies in our pocket, Rochelle Printing agreed to print the magazine for a half down at the time of shipment and 90 days credit on the second half. On our monthly schedule, this was eventually worth more than ten grand in credit to us. Sax at Rochelle was willing to go along because he'd just purchased a new press and needed work for it. More special timing.

Lucky break #3. *Empire News* took over our distribution and gave us more financial security. We got an especially good deal from them because we already had the 70,000 orders.

Lucky break #4. This one concerns Central Photo Engraving and it's a first-rate example of how we kept ▶

falling in, and coming out smelling like roses. I didn't have any contacts in the engraving field, so Johnny Mastro of Esquire *suggested three good houses and El went and talked to them. The first two offered good unit rates and credit. The third Johnny suggested was Central Typesetting, a big outfit that specializes in both type and engravings. When I looked up the address in the Yellow Book, I got "Central Photo Engraving" by mistake and had El go there. The place we picked by mistake gave us six months of engravings as an investment and tossed in $600 in cash.*

Lucky break #5. *This one is the topper. I think the name of a magazine is extremely important, because it can greatly aid or limit a publication's growth. I further feel that* Playboy *is the perfect title for our magazine and what we hope it will become—but we had to have the title* forced *on us. We were almost to press with the first issue and we were using the title "Stag Party." With the aid of hindsight, I can say with certainty that it would have been an extremely limiting name—particularly considering how well the magazine has been accepted as more than a girlie book. It took a threatening letter just before print time from the lawyers of* Stag *magazine to make us abandon "Stag Party"— though we'd all had reservations about that title for some weeks. Over a weekend we selected* Playboy *and the terrific rabbit symbol. I often think—what if* Stag *hadn't threatened us until after we'd published an issue or two under the "Stag Party" logo. Like I said, we've been lucky.*

*A*llow Yourself
to Feel Successful,
and You Will Be

It's all relative. I thought I was hugely successful in the first year of the magazine because I managed to get enough money to publish the second issue and the third. Then the letters started coming in from people applauding the concept of the magazine when it was still being put together with very little money. But what I couldn't possibly have imagined were the years that followed and what an empire it would become.

I felt as if I'd been born for it. I felt like Clark Kent going into that phone booth and then bursting out with that big S on his chest. When you accept that feeling, then you can believe a man can fly.

Through the Eyes of the Master: What to Look for When Looking at a Nude Photograph

It depends very much what you're looking for. First and foremost, you look at the face. Is she beautiful in the photo? Doesn't matter how nicely posed the rest of it is. If the face is good, then it's a matter of body attractiveness. One assumes before you're shooting a centerfold that she's a beautiful girl, but has the camera captured that? Throughout most of Playboy's *history, the centerfolds were shot with an 8 × 10 camera, which has a slow shutter speed, making it difficult to get spontaneity.*

The best poses are the ones that don't look too stiff, but should be able to make you stiff. That's about as good a credo as I can share.

*B*ad Times Remind You to Enjoy the Good Times

So many things can get you down. Then you start feeling sorry for yourself. But the reality is, if you wake up in the morning and you're alive and healthy and feel good about it, you're already far ahead of the game.

I have managed to remain optimistic during troubled times—not simply in terms of romance, but in terms of business and everything else—by the recognition that you can tell how good things are only by comparing them with when they weren't so good.

———

*Y*oung Dreams Will Age Well Along with You

You can give up and settle for less if that's what you want to do. What we call maturity, in many cases, is just compromise.

For me, my eternal optimism has seen me through. Much of it has to do with staying connected to the dreams of childhood, staying in touch with the boy I once was, and loving that boy and his dreams. It makes everything all the more satisfying. I could be living exactly the same life and be getting a lot less satisfaction out of it if I wasn't really still in touch with the innocent boy dreaming the dream.

———

He decided that he would forever live a boy's life, a boy's dream, so as to never become jaded or cynical. He would never allow himself to feel overly sophisticated. "I probably am today and will always remain a little bit of the youngster," he said long ago and evermore. "This is something that is too soon dead in most all of us, and I'm doing my best to keep it alive in me." He now wanders his large property and is truly touched by little things that remind him of his boyhood backyard—ants and butterflies and crickets, backyard stuff. Et cetera. And then he gets to go upstairs to his bedroom and see naked women waiting for him. He gets to see all the things his inner boy had dreamt of.

Try living such a life, and make millions while doing so, and see if the world doesn't come after you, looking for some retribution. It does, will, and certainly did. He would become among the most censored men in history—for daring to throw sex into sunlight, for pulling it out of shadows and alleys; a simple and revolutionary (and maybe healthy?) notion, since he was the first one to think of it, only to be persecuted for doing so forthrightly, on nice paper stock, accompanied by good literature and fine illustrations and urbane life advice. He was considered to be trouble, in a *Leave It to Beaver* era, and eras beyond. J. Edgar Hoover and the FBI started a file on him early on. Nixon later placed him on his enemies list. Meanwhile, the state of Illinois, the city of Chicago, the state of New York, the state of New Jersey, all of Great Britain—at one point or another, they all came after him to levy punishments of one kind or another, as it was clear that he threatened a puritanical morality that creaked, was on its last legs, especially as compromised Bible-thumpers of the religious right kept getting caught in bed with compromised ladies.

In the mid-eighties, Ronald Reagan's commission headed by Edwin Meese successfully managed to have his magazine banned from convenience stores. That encumbrance, as with all others before it, dissolved in short order, went away, not that the setback wasn't felt; he experienced a

minor stroke in March 1985. There were female problems in the same time frame as well, with an obstreperous Special Lady. Then he got back up and reconfigured his world. "I put down the luggage of my life," he said. "I quit burning my candle at both ends and started savoring every day."

*A*nd When All Is Seemingly Lost . . .

You just have to rise again. You have to keep getting up.

---

*F*riendships Last for a Reason

Making a friend for life is more a matter of what kind of a friend you are. You certainly in most cases can tell— you just connect on every level, especially in terms of shared interests and sensibilities.

But particularly when it involves the opposite sex, everything is not always out on the table, and you're never really sure. You may remain a friend for life, but platonic friendships tend to last longer than romantic connections.

He has often referred to those who are endlessly welcome at his home as the closely knit Family of Friends, aka The Gang. Their names are kept on the Gate List, permitting them access to the Master's Shangri-la at any time, although lately they mostly come when expected. (They announce themselves to a speaker embedded in a boulder at the main gate—the Talking Rock!—and security staff then triggers the lowering of the drawbridge.) In the old days, there would usually be a friend or several sleeping over—Tony Curtis, Shel Silverstein, the historian Max Lerner, et cetera—living in the house, enjoying semipermanent residence, sometimes recovering from addictions (or broken loves), taking meals, taking lovers, playing games all night with him, in case he felt the need.

A Chicago nightlife impresario who came to work for the Playboy Clubs, a sweet rogue named John Dante, for instance—he was one of the closest, one who would live in both houses, play games, and be an ever-present ear for Hef. In 1968, Dante began squandering money on football bets like never before, and suddenly he was in bookie hock for $38,000 and also mostly broke, and was therefore scared shitless of thugs looking for the return of green. (Dante was the sort of guy who talked like that, rest his soul.)

He would recall: "I didn't even want to think about how much I owed, but it was hanging over my head like a guillotine—and I knew that by Tuesday morning the calls would start coming in: 'Moe Gagliano is on the line from Denver,' and if I didn't take the call somebody would show up at the front door." (Don't swing, don't ring, please!) He somehow bought himself a week, only to get out of town, take the big powder, split from the company, the Mansion, the Life, completely on the q.t.—hey, maybe even sign on as a steward on an ocean liner bound for Italy, just to disappear. He said nothing to Hef, kept playing all-night Monopoly with him and laughing it up, but finally blurted the what-was-what to Hef's number one, secretary Bobbie Arnstein, telling her to keep mum, which she of course did not do.

"I was lying on my bed talking to myself when's there's a knock at the door," he said. "For a second I think it's *them*, but it's Hef, with a very somber expression on his face."

And so said Hef, walking in, sitting down, staring into his friend's red-rimmed eyes: "Let's talk. What happened?"

The whole story came out—or, well, *"I told him the whole fucking story,"* per Dante.

Said Hef: "Why didn't you come to me?" Then: "How much do you owe in all?"

The check was in Dante's hand the next day.

But before Hef left the room, he told the desperate and humbled and frightened associate: "Try not to do it again, John. You're too good a friend to lose."

And then Dante wept and wept. And wept a little more.

*Y*our Wedding Day Should Wait a While, for You

You don't really know who you are until your thirties. Most often, settling down with a mate at an earlier age is a mistake.

Ideally, young men—and women, too—ought to first spend some significant time away from home, living on their own as a single person to find out who they are and what they really want out of life.

If you put off making the commitment, you are more likely to stay committed longer.

While all too young, he knew not who he was, but had a feeling at the same time that he knew who he would someday become. He sensed something else was coming. Yet he conformed, for that minute. Did what he was supposed to do, for that minute, or for ten years of that minute, for as long as it would last. Still, where he was, June 1949, when he married Miss Millie Williams: "The thought of a young man simply moving out of his home and into an apartment and living as a bachelor and pursuing one's own aspirations was not an option in those days. Bachelors who were still unmarried in their thirties were suspect, and women in their thirties and unmarried were considered old maids. So in our early twenties, all of us got married at the same time. All my peers, my classmates, we got married within a year or two of one another. Thankfully, this doesn't have to happen anymore."

Hef Explains the Vagaries of Marriage

(AS ONLY HE CAN): A REQUIRED COURSE IN HUMAN CHEMISTRY

* *The most logical motivation for getting married is because you want to have children.*

* *A less logical motivation is for the emotional security of it, feeling that you won't be able to hold on to the relationship without marriage.*

* *Or you believe that it will somehow improve the relationship. That can also be a false premise.*

* *Some relationships improve with marriage, but a lot of them don't.*

* *The reason a lot of them don't is because people tend to get lazy in a relationship and don't work at it.*

* *The best relationships are those where both people are really trying to make it work.*

* *That should be a given in your marriage, but isn't always true.*

▶

- *You take it all for granted and forget the very reasons you fell in love to begin with.*

- *Remember, different people have different kinds of needs.*

- *In the very early stages of a romantic relationship—the first two or three years—there is something chemical going on in the body that feels like an amphetamine. A physical excitement.*

- *With the passage of time, that's replaced chemically by a more soothing feeling, like taking a tranquilizer.*

- *Some people are very happy with that second stage.*

- *They are the ones that are likely to be happy in terms of a long-term relationship.*

- *Others need that adrenaline fix.*

- *Those are the people who may not want to jump into marriage, because a seven-year itch or three-year itch or three-month itch will be waiting for you.*

- *It's all in the chemistry.*

Of course he did try it again. With Kimberley Conrad, whom he saw as an antidote to difficult times, a safe harbor after having ridden rough waves. He saw her wandering about his property, another lovely visitor staying in the Guest House, and he decided he wanted her as he hadn't wanted any other Special Lady ever before.

"Despite the age disparity, we enjoy the same kind of life," he had said. "She enjoys spending her evenings here with me and with friends and watching old movies and playing games and just being together." On the night of July 23, 1988—six months after their first night together, when she had agreed to begin to get to know him—he led her out of the Game House, where she had just beaten him at foosball, and over to the wishing well, where he did what he had not done since 1948, with Millie. He begged her hand in marriage. And Kimberley said, "Do I have to answer now?" And his jaw dropped. But she recovered within seconds and said, "Of course I'll marry you!"

The following July 1, they returned to the well and pledged their troth before friends and family. Then he became a father again, this time to two boys, Marston and Cooper, became settled and serene. But as these things happen, after ten years together, she somehow no longer enjoyed spending evenings watching old movies and playing games and experiencing the hurly-burly of Mansion activity—even though, as never before in his life, he remained true-blue faithful to her. So he bought her the

house next door, a two-and-a-half-acre property, and she and the boys moved. Not far, ever close and close to his heart, but moved.

He would say, "I think it's clear that being married—raising children, settling down—is not the answer for everybody. There are alternate ways of living your life, very ethical and appropriate ways." Meanwhile, he would have new romantic adventures to pursue, as only he could. He said, "If I had known what was waiting for me after the marriage, the marriage wouldn't have lasted as long as it did."

Part 5

INSIDE THE BEDROOM

Making Love Like the Master

How a sex god—well, how *the* sex god—became such: First, he was born into the most repressive of Midwestern households, wherein the subject of bodily functions of any sort incited great embarrassment. It was only during his army years that, at age nineteen, he learned to pleasure himself, an act that he had not yet fathomed to attempt. And so he came quite late to the party. There were females by then, and soon after, with whom he might have had his way, females other than the one he took as his fiancée, but he abstained conspicuously: "Although I'd had opportunities to go all the way with a couple other girls, I really didn't want to have sex with someone that I wasn't planning on marrying. In that sense, I was a very old-fashioned boy."

At such time, in fact, there was no play at all in the boy, just abject conformity to a rigid society that had long vexed him. What vexed next: After he and Millie at last achieved clandestine consummation (the aforementioned holiday in Danville, Illinois, whose sole purpose was, in short, Let's Get This Over With), and after she had graduated months before him to accept a teaching job elsewhere, she then proceeded to embark upon an affair with a high school coach. Once she confessed to it, Hugh Hefner's view of sex shifted completely—which eventually shifted the course of American sexuality every bit as completely. She told

147

him it had happened just one time, which squashed his heart entirely, but he learned years later that it was ongoing until weeks before they were wed. Still, he would recall: "I never doubted that I loved her or that I wanted to marry her, but things would never really be the same again. I sat alone in my room and tried to make some sense of it all, playing Billy Eckstine records like 'Fool That I Am.'" Also, he said: "This was the single most devastating experience of my life, and in a certain sense, I don't think I ever got over it." But they married nonetheless, which was what was supposed to happen. And only then, suddenly stifled by constraints of career and household, unable to forget Millie's indiscretion, objecting to a culture of sexual hypocrisy where blame was useless, because sexual adventure was forever to be the elephant in the room of life, he felt something snap inside, and he began to consider options, notions, possibilities, fantasies. He began to think randy thoughts he had not permitted himself to think before. High jinks ensued.

Other couples came to their stylish new apartment, whereupon he stylishly instigated new and extraordinary adult activities: "We'd play strip charades," recalled his childhood friend Janie Borson Sellers, who with her husband, Eldon, showed up regularly. "We were all experimenting. We played strip poker, strip spin the bottle. We were all married, but it was very arousing. I remember one time we watched a stag movie, the four of us on their big double bed, and we decided to make love, each to our own partner. It seemed natural. Hef suggested it." Said Millie, who gamely indulged the whims of her spouse, even though just a little concerned:

"He was the initiator of a lot of different things. Yet he was sensitive enough to know how to balance it with humor so that people would willingly partake. What he was reaching for was just under the skin of everybody, and he was the leader. I really had a sexual education and was probably lucky for having it. But I also thought, 'There's something wrong here when he needs to do all these new and kinky things.'"

Meanwhile, the leader himself would later proclaim: "It was the American fifties and I was suffocated and needed air. I was convinced that there was an exciting world out there and I wasn't part of it. I felt like an outsider without any real connections to a world I knew only in books and movies. I didn't want to grow up safe and sorry like my parents had."

*T*here Is a Message in a Bottle for You

The great myth about sex and sexual desires has always been that if you bottle them up, they won't bother you. The truth is, if you let those desires out and deal with them in a rational way, you'll be the happier for it.

What is the real message in a bottle? The message that society, church, and state have tried to suppress for so long is that sex isn't just for procreation and shouldn't be limited to marriage. It's a natural part of being alive. Embrace it and you embrace life itself.

The Female Body Is Aroused in More Than One Place

It all begins with what's on her mind, so it starts with the brain. After that, it's the clitoris. But each woman is different. You figure it out as you go. The nipples are erotic for some. And of course the lips and the small of the neck.

When I was growing up, they told you that the root to seduction was blowing in a girl's ear. I don't recommend it. You can spend a whole night blowing in a girl's ear without much more than her eventually saying, "There's a draft in here, darling."

Once the magazine was up and running in late 1953, so too was his libido, as never before. "Sex in the office was commonplace," he said. "We were on the cutting edge of a sexual revolution that wouldn't really hit mainstream America until the mid-sixties. If Kinsey had done the research, I was the pamphleteer, spreading the news of sexual liberation through a monthly magazine—but also living the life as well." (Paul Gebhard of the Kinsey Institute once admiringly noted: "Hefner's genius was to associate sex with upward mobility.")

Regularly, during staff meetings he would excuse himself when informed that a woman awaited him in his private office quarters. "Duty calls," he would announce to his small band of employees, then go take care of business before returning to the meeting, where he had also been taking care of business. "We'd sit there waiting for him while he got laid," said Arthur Paul, *Playboy*'s legendary art director, the man who also designed a rabbit-head logo that was to become instantly recognizable around the world. "We were envious as hell." Thus, the editor-publisher was never especially circumspect about his early dalliances. Said the magazine's first photo editor, Vince Tajiri: "I had the feeling he was proud of it, excited about making discoveries about sex. It liberated him. He was very open about it with me, which was surprising at a time when affairs were hushed-up experiences. I think he came to sex a little late, bumped into it, and then became obsessed with it."

Well, yes. And this was good, he said, and this was correct, he also said (if conducted openly and honestly and lovingly, he always said; he would end his marriage in 1957, after sharing such open honesty), and this was only where it began, really. The fire burned hard from then on. Author Gay Talese, in his 1981 landmark exploration of American sexuality, *Thy Neighbor's Wife,* described the life and mind of a forty-five-year-old Hefner, a Hefner who had by then slept with hundreds of nubile bedmates: "Each occasion with a new woman was for him a novel experience: It was as if he was always watching for the first time a woman undress, rediscovering with delight the beauty of the female body, breathlessly expectant as panties were removed and smooth buttocks were exposed—and he never tired of the consummate act. He was a sex junkie with an insatiable habit."

Well, yes.

*T*each Your Hands a Few Tricks

When I was young, women used to wear brassieres with double hooks on the back. I took some pride in the fact that I could reach back and, even through a sweater, flip the strap and unfasten the hooks. Of course, these days most women I date don't wear brassieres. Still, it's not a bad idea for a guy to keep in practice.

His hands would always be equal opportunity explorers, for certain. (It is said that his fingertips should one day be enshrined at the Smithsonian.) As the nineties dawned, however, a preponderance of silicone and saline graced his pages, and thus at decade's end, his love life. Rare was the new Playmate whose décolletage had not been reconfigured.

*T*he Handful Quandary:
Real Breasts Versus the Enhanced Version

There's no question that natural is better. But I think when Mother Nature hasn't taken care of business, a case can be made for improving the situation. First and foremost, for self-esteem. And a good breast job can look and feel quite natural.

―――――――

Incidentally, by the end of 2003, exactly six hundred Playmates had appeared in the magazine, wearing skimpy things and no things at all. Only because he was asked, he once said, "Just how many Playmates came to my bed over the years? There would be times, depending on what was going on, in which I would be romantically involved with maybe eleven of the twelve Playmates in a year. But of course there would be a time when ten went by and I wouldn't be involved with any of them."

To that end, this would be a good place to dispel one of the urban myths surrounding *Playboy:* the secret of the stars on the cover. "According to legend," he would reveal, "the number of little stars on the cover of each issue was a code for how I rated that cover girl or centerfold in bed. The stars actually represented regional editions for advertising purposes. But the myth began in the early sixties and we didn't attempt to discourage it. It had become so widespread that they satirized it on *Saturday Night Live* when I hosted the show in 1977. Sometime in the seventies, we discontinued the regional editions and the stars became unnecessary. And I said, 'Just leave 'em on for a while.' It had, after all, become part of the mystique."

The More You Know, the More They Want You

A lack of experience may be attractive in women, but not in men. Although they say they like a one-woman man, most women are attracted to a man who has had a number of romantic relationships and knows his way around a bedroom. The more experienced you are, the more desirable you are to most women. If a woman knows that other women find you attractive, she is likely to find you attractive as well.

*L*acy and Racy Notions

I still find garter belts and stockings erotic—particularly with high-heeled shoes. The most enticing lingerie really comes from the thirties and forties. Lacy underwear is always attractive and very feminine. Still works for me.

---

*B*edroom Accessories Never Hurt the Cause

You obviously need sex toys. The Hitachi Wand vibrator is the most important one—it works, in fact, very much like a magic wand. Baby oil or K-Y jelly are essentials as well. I'm a visual guy, so I have a mirror on the ceiling. A large television screen is important for your X-rated videos. And I have a refrigerator in the bedroom, too, for refreshments.

He has always been legendary for his fondness for home gadgetry, and his bedroom has long known the purr of battery-powered foreplay, of pulsating electronically enhanced lovemaking. It was to be no other way. Plus, whenever the Bed was unusually crowded, the toys worked well to distract unattended-to participants. From one such participant: "Granted, when there are six girls and one guy, what are you gonna do? I think a lot of us liked playing with the vibrators, and there were a lot of times that's all you got."

Sometimes, too, quieter toys made an impact. For instance, the Killer Ben-Wa Balls Incident, a classic Mansion moment. One Special Lady had received a pair of Japanese ben-wa balls from a friend and, well, inserted them one evening and, well, forgot they were in place, forgot all about them. Hours later she found herself in the Bed astride, well, Hef's face while he pleasured her. "We were going at it," she recalled, "and all of a sudden he was shoving me off and gagging—*ack, ack, ack*—and I realized that they'd gone down into his throat. They almost killed him. I just kind of Heimliched him and got 'em out. It seemed funny afterward, and I had them framed with background of Purple Heart velvet and the motto LEST WE FORGET.'"

 Funny Thing Happens on Your Way to Love

If you don't see the humor in sex, you don't see the humanity in it. They go hand in hand.

And then there is the business of baby oil. No Mansion cupboard since the sixties has been devoid of it. Row upon row of Johnson's baby oil bottles standing sentry, awaiting the Master's next urge. In point of fact, the Chicago Mansion's

Round Rotating Bed headboard contained, in the far left corner, a plentiful stash of bottles. It is merely the stuff of slick sensual legend on his premises, and here is why: "Perhaps the only sexual quirk Hefner has is his fetish for baby oil," recalled Playmate Marilyn Cole. "He would spend hours rubbing it all over me like a master chef tenderly basting a chicken. It was his way of making me ready for him. It also had a somewhat unfortunate side effect. If a girl spends half the night getting covered in baby oil, she inevitably ends up with very greasy hair." Or from Playmate Marcy Hanson: "Oh, God, the baby oil! It's a bitch to get it out of your hair. It can take days and days. Each of us had her own way of getting it out—everything from champagne to baby powder to 'Fuck it, let's do it again.'"

To Serve and Protect Like a Man Requires Noticing

There are many forms of safe sex, and most have to do with really paying attention to what's going on related to your body and hers. I've never been a big prophylactic man, but I have never gotten a woman pregnant when I wasn't married and I've never had a problem with sexually transmitted diseases. It has to do with taking care of business.

Reflections on the Little Blue Pill

If you take Viagra one hour before the fact, it can last eight to twelve hours. I don't mean the sex can last eight or twelve hours, but the effect can. If you have seven girlfriends, let me say, you need *the little blue pill.*

Viagra isn't just for older guys. This pill is not for people of a certain age; this pill is for guys of any age. There's always a time when you're looking for wood—nights when you're drinking a lot, for instance—and it may not be there. It provides the certainty that wood is there when you need it.

He would declare Viagra the best gift he ever received. Never mind that his virile endurance has always been his pride and joy. One woman long ago said that he could go to it in such epic and extended fashion that it almost got "borin'." What man would not take that as praise?

As it turned out, this new gift arrived in his life precisely at the most opportune moment. His separation from Kimberley Conrad Hefner had been announced three months earlier, and in the tumultuous interim, he found himself to be hermetically unsealed, leaving the tall gates and stone walls behind, charting the new real world again—and discovering that young women were still as interested in him as he had always been in them. He said of that same moment: "So many young people were waiting for me to come out and play. It was like spotting Elvis at the supermarket."

And so on April 9, 1998—his seventy-second birthday, as spry and rejuvenating a birthday for him as ever before—new blue pharmaceutical magic was presented to him, because if not to him, then to whom? Never was there a more appropriate test pilot for such a blue-yonder flight. He flew and did not stop: "It redefines the boundary between fantasy and reality. I think Viagra is the best recreational drug in America." He would even share blue bounty, for experimental purposes, with the Ladies in his Bed. "They insisted," he said. "In theory, it should work as well for women as it does for men, but the results are thus far inconclusive. I think we need to do a little more research."

He always did know how to work it. Or play it.

*B*ut Staying Hard Without a Blue Pill
Needn't Be Hard to Do

Fear of premature ejaculation has never been part of my experience. I don't know what that's all about. One could argue that there is no such thing as premature ejaculation. When you want to ejaculate, you ejaculate. It may be premature for her, but not for you.

Conversely, however, that is part of what endurance is all about: You should be thinking about her pleasure and her climax. That actually does help you get to where you ought to be. Don't think about Mickey Mantle. Think about the girl you are with, not just about your own satisfaction.

---

*N*umbers Don't Matter

Part of my life has been a testing of the outer boundaries of sexuality, stretching the limits of what you can do and still consider yourself moral. Morality is not defined by numbers of partners. You can have sex with just one person and this can be a very immoral relationship.

People understood early on the kinds of parties he might wish to attend, this new renegade of bohemian upscale decadence—whatever such a thing could mean at such a time. "I went to my first orgy in 1957 on my first visit to Hollywood," he recalled. "It was a beatnik affair held in my honor at a home filled with models and starlets. It convinced me that everything about Hollywood that I ever fantasized about was true." A female participant in that event would, however, remember that when the night ended, there was Young Mr. Playboy, mogul in the making, curled up in front of a fireplace, nude, sleeping beside a cat. As in: These Things Take Practice. He practiced well and with vigor. At the Chicago Mansion, he practiced on the Round Bed with carefully selected partners—friends, eager dormitory Bunnies, and others. Then he moved practice downstairs to his enormous Roman bath, where bubbles would foam and soft music would play and there would never be fewer than ten women to four guys—the Hefner ratio, this, and only because of utter trust in the other guys. Some pairings would then wander a few yards away from the bath and over to the water bed—among the first such undulating sleep mats in the world—and continue what had already begun amid wet soap. (Quoth Dean Martin, during an NBC-TV Hef roast: "He gets so much action, he's got the only water bed with whitecaps.") Said John Dante, his Playboy Club executive and Monopoly pal, and one of the trusted chosen in group experimentations, back then and thereafter: "We had a ball.

You'd be kissing one girl—kissing two. You'd have two lovely faces on either side of you, God almighty—it was the most fantastic happening you can ever imagine—beautifully made up, one more gorgeous than the other, perfectly formed bodies, stroking you, sucking you, fucking you. But Hef was the main thing. He was playful about it all. It was strictly fantasy time, indulging all of the senses from food to smell to taste. He enjoyed seeing all of us get pleasure—men and women alike. How bad can that be?"

Such scenes became almost a Mansion West constant beginning in late 1976, upon the final departure of Barbi Benton, who had never been inclined to play with others. "Hef used to ask me if I was ever interested in having a third party join in," she would recall, "and I had no interest in that—guys or girls, for my birthday or his. No way." He took on his newfound liberation with blissful abandon: "I was more committed than ever to noncommitment. This was my real swing period. It was not simply a third girl, but every variation on a theme—and I do mean everything imaginable in the realm of experimentation. We literally had a little community of group sex, a circle of a dozen friends who were into scenes."

Thus was born the eternal Mansion mystique, wherein anything could happen and usually did—but only if you wanted it to. Still, he was always gentle and deferential, concerned about the feelings of those who partook and those who did not. "Sex was never mandatory with Hef," said Playmate Monique St. Pierre. "It was always optional. It wasn't as if he didn't have enough women." Still, players who played during that halcyon playtime uniformly wax wistful about it: "It was just a fabulous time of free love," said Marcy Hanson. "Everything you read about or thought about really did happen. But in such a loving way. It wasn't seedy, like when you think of Larry Flynt or that other jerk, Guccione."

The More Can Very Much Be the Merrier

Women come to me with the expectation of having multi-partner sex, but that's more true today than at any other time in my life. Before that, I certainly discussed with girls that I was dating the possibility of bringing other women to our bed. But it's something that you can do only as long as both you and she are comfortable with it.

It's a big mistake to get into multi-partner relationships if there isn't real understanding and security in the primary relationship. You need to be sure, I think, not only that you're going to feel fine the following day, but that she will, too. It's foolish to squander the tomorrows that exist in a relationship for a momentary adventure. It's not a smart way to live your life.

I've always felt, quite frankly, that it's a mistake to put off pleasure, but I think you should do it rationally. You should live for today and also for tomorrow.

A Mansion orgy, then, was always happily consensual, full of good cheer and humor, lacking inhibition and later regret. Still, while all involved were sating each other, the gratification of one in particular was understandably paramount. "The girls all loved Hef and wanted to make him feel like a sultan," said John Dante, who witnessed much as well as participated frequently. He once recalled a vigorous roundelay in the sprawling Master Bed during which eight females had come to play with the Master and Dante and another fortunate friend. And it was good. As it always was. And it was crowded, as it often was: "Everybody was on top of everybody else. You didn't know who was where." And it was an hour on, as it also often was. And Dante was atop a female, deeply in flagrante delicto, as it were. As was the Master, somewhere else amid the scrum. "All of a sudden, I hear, *'Uhhh, uhhh, uhhh!'* Hef is about to go. All of the girls in the bed, including the one that's under me, start saying, 'Come on, Hef! C'mon, baby! Come on!'" Which is exactly what then did occur, as it always did. "And all the girls are laughing, including the one under me. I look into her face and go back to what I was doing with her. And she looks at me, and what I read in her face is, 'Hey, schmucko, it's over!'" So she disengaged from Dante while remaining beneath him, while the Master called downstairs for food. "And she says to him, with me on top of her still, 'I'll have a cheeseburger and a malted milk.' Hef repeats in the phone, 'One cheeseburger, one malted milk.' And that was it. After Hef came, it was over.'"

There Are No Guidebooks for Swinging, So Proceed with Caution

If there are any rules of etiquette in having consensual multi-partner sex, I haven't found them yet. Just pay attention to what's going on around you and don't do anything you'll feel guilty about the next day.

For one who never learned to swim, he would commune in water more famously than most. But then he had created perhaps the most famous Grotto in modern civilization in order to achieve that distinction. Plus, as he would point out, "You don't swim in the Grotto. It's all standing, sitting, and lying down." It is all that and human wave making. It is the Jacuzzi of all Jacuzzis, the cave of love, hidden behind a waterfall, connected to the pool via an underwater tunnel, and yet separate unto itself because of its legendary frolics. Secreted away in the stone walls are five synthetic boulders that pipe intimate music—the singing rocks!—while those who swirl in the warm waters make beautiful music. Upon obtaining his Shangri-la in Holmby Hills, he decreed that a Grotto was required and that it be constructed to resemble something that "had emerged from the sea millions of years ago," according to its architect, Ron Dirsmith. "When it was finished, it had an ethereal,

Hef's

LITTLE BLACK BOOK

timeless quality, almost like being in some kind of church. Hef related to it *philosophically*. It was a very serious moment." And then the sex started.

rotto Love Has Its Ups and Downs

In a certain sense, it's like making love in a steam bath. The heat and humidity are nice initially but it limits your potential. Certain women, however, have expressed great fondness for the water jets. Historically, most of the lovemaking I've done in the Grotto has been foreplay that then led to the bedroom.

Oftentimes whenever sex started in his bedroom at either Mansion, he would flip a switch and a video camera—embedded in the wall, trained upon the action—began to capture the magic unfolding. He was always one to document his life, after all. "Early on, in a gadget-filled house, I recorded a lot of sexual adventures," he would say, "but only with the participants' knowledge and approval." (After the technology had advanced, he and his partners could actually watch themselves carry on while they carried on, which did require a good amount of neck-craning.) As he is who he is, voyeuristic proclivities such as these were his birthright, except he didn't know it until his libido awoke during his marriage to Millie. It was in that period he asked his father to buy him a 16-millimeter projector for Christmas; his father would never suspect why, nor would Millie—until frequent screenings of stag films became part of their home entertaining. In no time, he became a connoisseur of the genre, as primitive as it was then. Duly inspired, just before starting a magazine that would embrace all things racy, he and his friend Eldon Sellers made their own stag film, very much on the sly, with a willing young woman.

Sellers, who was merely the accomplice, would recall: "He asked me to be involved, and I was all for it. It was his idea to call it *After the Masquerade Ball*. We wore masks—it was the funniest thing. Despite the masks, Hef was worried about someone recognizing him someday. So he asked me if I would take his place in close-ups—trade places with him, including some of the sex scenes, even though he was in ninety percent of them. Hef could talk anybody into anything if he tried."

*T*he Best Adult Videos Are All About You

The most erotic films, first of all, don't have much plot and, second of all, have everything to do with the attractiveness to you of the participants and the attractiveness to you of the nature of the sexual activity.

———————

As for the status of his vast library of Mansion Bedroom home videos, the news should sadden certain historians: "I got rid of them in the eighties. I thought it was time and didn't want them falling into the wrong hands. Some of the women on the tapes were married with children by then, so we deep-sixed the tapes. Dumped them in the ocean. And even I don't know the location. The tapes are gone, but the memories linger on."

Keep the Sandman in His Proper Place

It's a good idea not to fall asleep while you're actually having intercourse. Not very polite. It's not a good idea to fall asleep in the middle of a conversation with a girlfriend, either.

You Need to Wake Up the Morning After the First Night with Some Class, Boys

Who was it that said that five minutes after he had sex, he wished the woman would turn into a poker table and five of his buddies?

I don't agree. The period after orgasm—if you're with somebody you care about—is a very sweet time. Cuddling is very important. In the morning, if it's someone you've just been with for the first time, the last thing a girl wants to hear is "I'll call you" when she thinks it's not true. If it's the first time, then what is looked for afterward is something sweet and romantic and reassuring, just the way it was before the sex.

---

*H*ef's Requisite Postcoital Meal

What I have to eat in the middle of the night, following sex: eggs sunny side up, with bacon, crisp. Hash brown potatoes. Buttered toast, grape jelly, a cold glass of milk, and applesauce. Followed by French toast. All served on a bed tray after sex, and then I sleep like a baby.

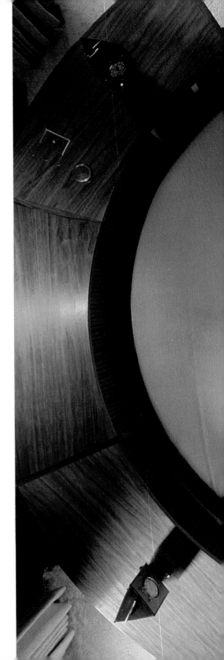

EPILOGUE

*How to Live Long
and Influence Playboys*

Mortality is the most unfair thing on the planet. All that makes it bearable is that it's universal. Still, there's a certain inequity in terms of when your time is up.

Truly, the key to longevity is taking care of yourself. But first and foremost, pick your parents with great care. Because if your parents live a long time, chances are you will, too. Also, stay out of hospitals. People die there.

To be Hef has ever been to defy odds. It is all in the genes. He came from strong genes, ones that encode long life. His mother lived to be a hundred and one years old. That alone would give him special hubris regarding mortality. His lifestyle gave him even more hubris in that regard: "Age is largely a number. If you are healthy, then how old you are has very little meaning." In his seventh decade, after siring two fresh scions, after surviving a marriage that came apart, he would begin to sow oats anew, begin dating again, be seen out painting the City of Angels crimson, clubbing, as they say, be seen out dancing and dancing, and then dancing some more, with young, beautiful women. As he would say: "My life is every bit as good and maybe even a little better in my seventies than it has been in the decades past. That thought would have been inconceivable to me when I was younger. My golden years have really turned out to be *the* golden years." He laughs last.

Shel Silverstein on Explaining Why Hef Will Never Die

DEATH GOES
TO THE MANSION

The late irrepressible poet, artist, singer, and longtime Playboy *contributor—and beloved Mansion habitué—Shel Silverstein often spun yarns during board-game marathons and once, in the late sixties, crafted an extemporaneous lark about what would happen if the Grim Reaper dared to turn up at the doorstep of the Chicago Mansion, looking for the proprietor—the playboy of playboys who kept strange, impossible hours and had a famous dislike for keeping business appointments.*

According to Silverstein, it would go something like this (as cribbed from an interview of long ago):

Well, it had to happen: It's time for Hef to die. So Death comes to the Chicago Mansion and rings the bell. The butler answers the door and asks, "Is Mr. Hefner expecting you?"

"No, but I think he'll see me," Death tells him.

▶

"I'm sorry, but Mr. Hefner's not available now," the butler says. "He's busy. But feel free to leave any correspondence at the Playboy Building, and it'll get to him."

After hearing more protestations, after clearing it with Hef, the butler lets Death in. Dressed in full fatal shroud, Death enters, checks his scythe at the door, and sits down, waiting for Hef.

"Mr. Hefner was expecting you, after all," the butler tells him, "but he's been up for seventy-two hours straight and needs more sleep. He'll be out in a couple of hours."

Three hours later, the butler calls for Death, who's been watching staff going in and out of Hef's room carting trays of peanut butter sandwiches and mashed potatoes with gravy. Butler says, "Mr. Hefner is now looking at a movie that he really wanted to see, but he said he will be out as soon as the film ends. In the meantime, would you like a drink?"

Death says, "Well, I'll take some Cognac."

And the butler brings Death some Cognac.

Four hours and twelve Cognacs later, Hef emerges from his quarters. He says, "Buddy, I really am sort of tied up right now. But I'd love to sit down with you first thing in the morning. Grab something to eat. Play some music. Use the pool. Meet the girls. Have a good time."

Death, now more than a little smashed, takes Hef's advice and goes downstairs to the pool. He takes off his Reaper cloak and sends it through the house laundry service, where it's immediately ironed. (This is Mansion Life, after all.) Meanwhile, the Mansion staff sharpens his scythe and stains the handle mahogany to match the rest of the house's décor.

Soon, it's time for the Bunnies to return from the Playboy Club. They jump in the pool, and Death swims nude with them, then starts ordering himself steak and champagne. Death is living the good life and thrilled about it. It's what we do here.

Months and months and months go by. Death has long made himself at home at Hef's. He's beside himself with happiness, living in the Leather Room, dating Bunnies, swacked on Cognac and champagne daily.

Death finally bumps into Hef, having forgotten why he ever showed up. Hef says, "So you're having fun, I hope." Death, bleary-eyed, just smiles and orders another steak and another bottle of champagne and goes back to his room.

Moral: The world of Hugh M. Hefner can seduce even Death. Because his world is all about Life.

ACKNOWLEDGMENTS

Very special gratitude is due to Mauro DiPreta, Joelle Yudin, Kim Lewis, Lorie Young, and Amy Hill at William Morrow; to Elizabeth Georgiou and the staff at *Playboy*'s Chicago Photo Library; to flawless archivist Steve Martinez at Playboy Mansion West; and to Josh Schollmeyer for his bravura editorial support throughout.